A Walk Down Memory Lane

Edited by Claire Tupholme

anchorbooks

*Poetry by the People
for the People*

anchorbooks

First published in Great Britain in 2007 by:
Anchor Books
Remus House
Coltsfoot Drive
Peterborough
PE2 9JX
Telephone: 01733 898102
Website: www.forwardpress.co.uk

SB ISBN 978-1 84418 467 5

Foreword

Anchor Books is a small press, established in 1992, with the aim of promoting readable poetry to as wide an audience as possible.

We hope to establish an outlet for writers of poetry who may have struggled to see their work in print.

The poems presented here have been selected from many entries, and as always editing proved to be a difficult task.

I trust this selection will delight and please the authors and all those who enjoy reading poetry.

Claire Tupholme

Editor

Contents

The Poems

Memories

Childhood days and childhood ways
Children's laughter in the street
Hopscotch chalked upon the pavement
All to test the skills of youth.

Cricket played against the gable
Fish and chips and your ginger pop
Liquorice and sherbet suckers
From the local corner shop.

Skipping girls who chant together
To the rhythm of the rope
Roller skating in the school yard
Aided by its gentle slope.

Children round a barrel organ
Listen to the merry tune
Coloured marbles in a gutter
On a sunny afternoon.

Ice cream from a horse-drawn vendor
Just a penny for a cone
Milk delivered in the morning
Straight into your jug or basin
By the milkman at your door.

Picking bluebells in the spinney
Catching minnows in the stream
Bread and jam upon the doorstep
All are part of childhood's dream.

Janet Cavill

Memory Lane

As we are left with memories dear,
Christmas to remember is the best time of the year.
Returning to a house and garden I well remember,
The date I recall was the 25th of December.
Walking down memory lane by the garden wall,
There stands a fir tree growing tall.
Once decorated and with presents on the front room floor,
Also a faithful old dog asleep by the door.
Christmas came and the twelve days went,
To us the life of that tree was not spent.
So we planted our tree by the garden wall,
To let it grow erect, fine and tall.
Memories like this of a Christmas past,
Will stay with you while life shall last.
Children do not mean to be unkind,
They make their own way in life, leaving us behind.
They do what they think is best,
Like swallows they spread their wings then leave the nest.
It seems unfair to put it mild,
Along life's way one has to lose a child.
You see Joseph and Mary as we all know,
They lost their child many years ago.
Our faithful dog grew old and his eyes grew dim,
So we had to say 'goodbye' to him.
He's as happy now as he's ever been,
Romping in paradise in pastures lush and green.
He's laid to rest by the stream with its gentle flow,
Under the old oak tree where the snowdrops grow.
I paused a while by the window I know,
To see happy children with their faces aglow.
They also have a decorated tree on the front room floor
And a faithful old dog asleep by the door.
As if turning back my life's pages it is now time to go,
So I turned away as it has started to snow.

I must not cry, I must be bolder,
Then someone shook me by my shoulder.
Saying, 'Wake up Gran, you've been dreaming I should say,
Wake up Gran, it's Christmas Day.'
And there the Christmas tree stood on the floor
And our faithful old dog asleep by the door.

Tom Basford

Wheeler-End

I love every blade of grass
Every leaf on every tree
I love every winding path
Through ferns so tall
Ferns seem even taller
When you are so small.
This special place is part of me
A mould in the ground
Where the duck pond used to be
A reminder of what was there, previously.
Memories of skating on thin ice
Warned not to go there
But would still entice.
I am often drawn back to roam
And see, a little girl there
That once was me.
There is nothing like it, I have found
To return to one's birthplace
To walk again on
One's home ground.

Janey Wiggins

Memories Of Uttoxeter

Of Uttoxeter memories the Butter Market springs to mind,
Rabbits, vegetables, flowers etc were sold, all of a different kind.
Miss Phillips' hat shop was such a treat,
When one had searched for a hat, hers couldn't be beat.

Carter Street housed Miss Beetham's art shop,
But Mrs Sampson's sweets further down were a certain stop.
Go to the Square and Ta-ta- Shaw's window always gave us a laugh
To read his clothes notes and not by half.

When we walked into Williamson's the grocery smell was so nice
Before crossing over to Copes for that extra slice.
Waiting for a winter train was quite at leisure
As the waiting room fire was such a pleasure.

I remember the cash travelling the wires in the Co-op shop,
The change was whizzed back, there was no need to stop.
In Balance Street where, on a Wednesday, the buses had to park
Some went early so it was up with the lark.

Talk of Balance Street, the church processions we had were a joy,
So proud to walk were every girl and boy.
Boots Library had some very good books,
Whether it be adventure or recipes for cooks.

Memories of Uttoxeter, this historic town and quite a retirement place,
For anyone who cares to come life would be at a slower pace.
The Heritage Centre houses all the facts of our town
Which, in Staffordshire, is of large renown.

Monica Baxter

I'll Never Forget . . .

'You'll be fine,' Mum told me as we got to the station,
'It's like a holiday, called evacuation.'
I was only five and did not understand,
I just didn't want Mum to let go of my hand.

'There'll be lots of children, you'll be able to play.'
I don't want to do that, I just wanna stay.
A lady came over and said, 'Hurry dear,
Just say goodbye cos the train's nearly here.'

She picked up my suitcase and told me to follow,
I was crying so much I just couldn't swallow.
It seemed like hours I was on that train,
When would I see Mum and Dad again?

We passed lots of fields, even saw my first cow
Then arrived at a halt, what happens now?
We were given some milk and nice biscuits too
Then a lady called out, 'I think I'll have you.

We'll go to my house now and that's where you'll stay
Till the nasty old bombs are all driven away.'
'If you don't mind please, I'd rather go home.'
'Now, now, dear don't fret, you won't be alone.

There are five other boys in the house where'll you stay
So I hope you'll be good and not get in my way.'
My bedroom was small, just a cupboard and bed,
Oh how I wish I was home instead.

'Come along dear, it's time for your tea.'
I wish I knew what was happening to me.
'Now, these are the boys dear, they're sort of your brothers.'
I ran back to bed and hid under the covers.

Because I was hungry I came back downstairs
And was greeted with giggles and lots of odd glares.
The food on the plate looked like soggy stew,
'Now eat it all up dear, what's wrong with you?
People are starving and that's all I've got
So you'll finish it up, if you like it or not.'

After a fortnight of just settling in,
Still not eating a lot and getting quite thin,
'I can't manage your curls dear,' she told me one day
So she cut them all off and threw them away.

Trudging down the lane with a slow approach
I saw people waving to me from a coach,
At first I could not believe my eyes,
It was Mummy and Daddy, oh what a surprise.

'Have you come to collect me? I'll just get my case.'
And I ran down the road at a very fast pace.
They looked quite shocked, that was plain to see,
'Aren't you eating darling, you look thin to me
And where are your curls? You had lovely hair.'
'Oh please take me home, Mum,' I cried in despair.

'I'll never be naughty, I'll never be bad,
I'll be the best child that you've ever had.'
The afternoon quickly came to an end,
They promised that lots of letters they'd send.

So I settled down to my old routine,
Not eating a lot and feeling unclean.
My hair kept itching, it looked a disgrace
Then spots appeared on my hands and my face.

Walking down the lane, I got to a gate
When a voice behind me yelled, 'Wait, darling, wait.'
It was Daddy who said, 'What's happened to you?
You don't even look like the girl I once knew.

I'm taking you home, bombs or no bombs, my dear
So let's get your things and get out of here.'
. . . All this happened sixty-five years ago
But I wanted to share it so you would all know

That so many children have been where I've been
Without having counsellors recreating the scene.
The war nearly brought Britain down to its knees
So why no reunion for us evacuees?

Mauren Milton

Carefree Memories

G aribaldi boys sharing the fun
  of carnival days, in rain or with sun
R egent, Regal, Gem, Empire too
  Aquarium, Plaza, for pictures we'd queue
E xcellent pier shows, brass bands were the craze
  fireworks exploding set warm nights ablaze
A erial circus, with bi-planes galore
  thrilling the crowds that were lining the shore
T he Forward and Back boats, boarded with laughter
  return trips to Gorleston, chats with the Master

Y acht pond bustling, dads with their nippers
  sailing their models of steamers and clippers
A quatic galas in the 100-yard pool
  with those 'Crazy Divers' acting the fool
R ide in a brake with horses of four
  an evening at Ormesby plus a nice country tour
M arina, a building, open-aired for the sun
  Neville Bishop and Wolves leading the fun
O ff from the beach for a family sea trip
  around Scroby Sands and St Nicholas lightship
U pwards we went on the tower (we felt brave)
  the revolving cage views of sea, country gave
T hrilling, the rides enjoyed in the speedboats
  tearing through waves but huddled in raincoats
H appy days, carefree memories forever
  a town of delight, Great Yarmouth, remember?

Roy Hacon

Nostalgia

Years ago when I was young
Oh many years ago
Things were very different then
The pace of life more slow

We didn't drive around in cars
For they cost so much money
And money's what we didn't have
So we went by shank's pony

We played at shops and whipping tops
And other childhood games
And when we had a falling out
We called each other names

And dressing up was so much fun
In Mother's old net curtain
Then we'd sing here comes the bride
And the groom was very uncertain.

The games we played were simple then
Like hopscotch and cat's cradle
We'd play until our mum called out
'Your tea is on the table'

At the sweet shop down the road
We'd spend our weekly coppers
On cherry lips and sherbet dips
Liquorice laces or gobstoppers

That's how it was those years ago
No computer or PlayStation
But we were never bored because
We used our imagination.

Ivy Nichols

Memory Lane

Me and my family lived along Memory Lane
There were just a few cottages and none were the same
Surrounded by acres of green fields and clear trout steams
So many friends and neighbours to share our sorrows and dreams

There were many times we were sent to school in our bare feet
And having enough to eat was a very rare treat
We went scrumping for apples, poached rabbit and trout
Our games were illegal of that I've no doubt

My mother was worried in case we got caught
With no money in her purse nothing could be bought
Fr Murphy was called in and made us confess
He gave absolution, some sweets and said, 'God bless.'

But she did her best to teach us right from wrong
And remind us that to our homeland we'd always belong
Our family was close and we loved one another
Especially the head of the household, our widowed mother

But our country was poor and we had to emigrate
And to our bosses we were most subordinate
As we were forced to take up the builders' great hod
And heave with our shoulders to turn over the sod

For there was no gap year in those days long ago
When Ireland's economy was on a go-slow
I sometimes look back at the poverty of those days before I left
When I hugged my tearful mother who felt so bereft

I wasn't the only one forced to leave my home
When the Irish were forced around the world to roam
In order to put some bread on the table
To keep those at home who were less able

When pay-day came we gladly sent home some money
To help feed our young siblings with bread but no honey
Now Ireland has become a very prosperous place
It's now a world leader in the economy race
Oh how I remember how we showed everyone great respect
And in gratitude for my mother's teaching, I genuflect.

Elizabeth Farrelly

A Walk In The Forest

We walked and talked as forest path we tread
of times when men worked the great forest for their bread
In Gloucestershire's great Forest of the Dean
ancient working sites can still be seen
Verderers and Kings and those men of yore
did sow and reap and mine the forest spore
men dug by candlelight till found
all the gifts of coal from underground
the mighty oaks from leafy glade
seamen sailed the ships from them made
oh, wondrous acres of the wild
such beauty is of nature's child
young trees now grow in brackens' bower
wild foxglove in its summer flower
but where the fallow and the roe
to follow wild boar soon you go
will the birds above know what is planned
and how long this great Forest of Dean will stand?

J Clarke

For All Seasons

In springtime, just as lovers should
We wandered hand in hand whene'er we could
In woods and fields and country lanes
In warm sunshine, wind or rain
Thanking God for all His gifts
Together loving.

In summertime a change of mood
Still together there we stood
Beside the stream, 'mong leafy bowers
Or in a garden, full of flowers
Thanking God, as so we should
Together sharing.

Autumn colours, green and brown
In golden sunshine, all around
Followed by winter's ice and snow
Setting hands and face aglow
We thanked God for all His gifts so good
Together still.

Dolly Harmer

I Wish To Sleep

I look at the river's gentle flow
Rippling quietly
Knowing what way to go
The sun beaming
Rays sparkling
Onto the water I start dreaming
This Earth I've found
Heaven
I see my only love, whisper thy sound
Oh why did I let you disappear
As the river proceeds
With not a hint of fear
So simple its journey
I want
Flowing gently without a sigh
Sunrays liquefied
I sit and wonder why
Was loving you
To be so painful
That everything looks much simpler
Now I wish this river was so deep
That I could follow the rays
And sleep.

Gareth Culshaw

Time To Dance

Weighing in at 130 pound
Our whirling dervisher could always be found.
In the darkest depths of old Soho
At a place well known, 'The Club Flamingo'.
If as a honky you ventured in
Your breath was taken by the noise and the din.

Black as the coals as you peered through its night,
There amongst the dancers, a *star* oh so bright.
With bouffant hair piled high as the fashion,
Dress stylish and trendy, she's moving with passion.
Lost in the music, she hasn't a care,
Long gone are the doubts that she shouldn't be there.

With Cleo her soulmate, this domino pair
Are dancing to Davis' latest jazz air,
There's no need to worry, this world is sublime
Its fun and its noise, its souls keeping time.

Charles Keeble

My Family Memory Lane

Time on your hands you have time to think
Of memories through your life
Some of joy, some of sadness
But one's life is never without fear
Mine was a family, five girls and two lads
A mum and dad any child could be proud of
They worked so hard each day of their lives
Most of the time they were not well
They never grumbled or complained
Times were hard but we never went without
There were always vegetables and fruit
Home-made bread, tarts and cakes
Lovingly made with their care
I was the youngest, I know I was spoilt
The older ones bought and made a fuss of me
The day I started school I did not want to leave my mum
I think she was sad as well
Through the years we all grew up
Gradually they married and left
But one thing in mind, they never forgot our dear parents
                                            who were so kind
Sad when Dad passed, Mum was on her own
When finally she too passed, life was never the same
Sadly our memories live on, we can never forget
I am the only one left now.

Eileen Finlinson

Friendship

She was my friend, she knew me through and through
And yet she took a loving view
Of my misgivings and my misdemeanours.
We had so many laughs together, so much fun
When we were young.
Shared interests of ballet, music and the theatre
Continued all our lives and though our paths diverged
We met to share remembrances.
To smile about our youth. Now she is gone,
Taking with her those long-past days
When we were young.

Christina Stowell

Little Paws

When I see the grass so green
In our garden you are there
No more ruts or holes are seen
Just our pup without a care.

When I see the old scratched door
In the kitchen you are there
Door now painted, sparkling white
Nosed open, how I stare.

When I see the collar hung
In the hallway you are there
Excitedly jumping up and down
Now the wall is sadly bare.

When I see the carpet down
In the lounge you are there
Nudging gently at my leg
No more to clean up hair.

When I see your loving face
In the photo you are there
You are with us little paws
You are everywhere.

C M Armstrong

So Long Ago

We were poor in pocket like most other folks
But we had good fun all the same.
Dad made us great toys from old bits of wood
Mum baked cakes on an old stone range.
We had hot buttered scones on cold winter nights
And candles in jars were our old cottage lights.
My home sweet home, a wonderful sight -
That was some years ago!
With the cottages gone and life moved on
I still feel a magical ray
From this small piece of heaven - surely God-given
To be cherished with each passing day.
Sometimes a teardrop falls from my eyes
As I glance at the photos of old
But they're tears of great joy which remain in my heart
Of sweet memories of so long ago.

Marian Theodora Maddison

I Remember Love

I remember love
A simple touch
A smile, a glance
The warmth of greeting
Shared thought, few words
Heart spoke to heart

I remember love
A sunset, darkening sky
Candles and a meal
Quiet conversation, sympathetic service
The wine we shared
Soft summer light
The perfume of you.

I remember love
Silence shared
No words needed
I remember love.

Geoffrey Speechly

Childhood Home

It was a small and happy house
With a huge garden with fruit trees
Also a few pigeons, rabbits and chickens
In this garden I had my special enclosure
On both sides were two scented lilac trees
With a stunning border of purple irises
In the back, one old bench with a barrel for a table
In the middle, an old-fashioned swing
Where I swung, sang and dreamt
It was my refuge, my own oasis

No, my house was not in the countryside
It was in the middle of the industrial city
From the house we could see the chimneys
Splashing their orange, white and black smoke
Arrogantly toward the sky
It was also the noisy characteristic sound
Of the melted ore poured in tanks' wagons

It was my great-grandparents' house
Lots of generations had lived in this house
Alas, I am the last one to live there
Because the house does not exist anymore
The front house was in the way for a larger road
All that's left, a large hole with a wild garden behind
And also, all my dreams of a young girl.

Victorine Lejeune Stubbs

The Garden Party

The ladies with their lacy gloves
And flimsy parasols
Trip lightly out across the lawn
Looking just like dolls.

Pink chiffon and motifs sweet
Etched upon their gowns
Beautifully stitched and patterned
The finest to be found.

Their straw hats decked with bows and flowers
And swathes of floaty tulle
As they flutter fast their painted fans
In an effort to keep cool.

The tables laid with crisp white cloths
And linen doilies too
The serviettes embroidered
With many a brightly hue.

The milk jugs covered over
With cloths all edged with beads
Sponge fingers in the trifle
And cakes with sesame seeds.

Tiny sandwiches of cucumber
Crab paste and buttered bread
'Hundreds and thousands' on the sponge
To enhance the tempting spread.

The young folk playing croquet
Or doing cartwheels on the green
A 'Lucky Dip' in the sawdust tub
All add sparkle to the scene.

Contentment shone and joys abound
In each gentle smiling face
In those days of yore when time stood still
And all was peace and grace.

Mollie D Earl

A Seaside Trip With Nan - A Monologue

When Nan took me and Butch out for the day
We'd end up on the train down Southend way
From Southend station we'd walk to the prom
And pick out which rides we'd like to go on
In Peter Pan's playground we'd spend an hour or three
While Nan sat down and drank her flask of tea
We rode the Jigsaw Railway and Noah's Ark
And all the other attractions in the park
We'd go and get some fish and chips to eat
And Rossi's ice cream made the perfect sweet
Nan had fourteen cups of tea to drink
Then we sunbathed till we all turned pink
We rode the little train out on the pier
We wandered off till Nan yelled out, 'Come here!'
Our speedboat ride set Nan back two-and-six
Poor Butch, not good in boats, was very sick
When we got back to the beach once again
The beach was wet, the tide had come right in
We donned our trunks and plunged into the wet
Nan hired a fourpenny deckchair, sat and slept
While me and Butch went splashing in the sea
Nan drank her way through eighteen cups of tea
The beach where we were swimming was Thorpe Bay
Another round of ice creams made our day
As we ambled back later, we had hot dogs and chips
From afar, you'd hear the smacking of our lips
We tried out all the slot machines, lights flashed and bells would ring
But all the way along the front, we never won a thing
We trudged all up Pier Hill to reach the High Street once again
We had half an hour to kill before catching our train
Nan found a little cafe and she said, 'Right, come with me.'
It must have been an hour since she'd had a cup of tea!
I bet you'd float a battleship in all the tea Nan drank
I never liked tea very much, it tasted really rank
I'm sure that Nan made sloshing sounds as we walked to the station
But after all we'd eaten, we couldn't begrudge her lubrication

We'd had a crackin' time all day before we left Southend
We all stood on the station, watched our train come round the bend
Once back at Nan's, we watched our favourite programmes on TV
And then our auntie brought us in some fish and chips for tea!

Mick Nash

My Memories

I remember all the good times of so very long ago
The times you watched me making snowmen, in the cold, cold snow
The secrecy of your Xmas presents was all a playful game
That special look of wonder when Father Xmas came
The fun we had on holidays, sleeping in a tent
A campsite near Caernarfon was usually where we went
Walking around the castle or playing on the beach
They weren't very far away, within easy reach
These are the very happy years, I remember so well
Whether you all feel the same, I don't know, I can't tell
The years have passed so fast, you are all now fully grown
The time came for you to leave and live lives of your own
Now you have your own children to make happy and to play
Life has gone full circle, it should be that way
I love you all, more than you can ever relate
That is what is written, that is my fate.

A Jones

Untidy Hazel

I can hear my dad shout up the stairs,
'My girl, are you getting up today?
Come clear up this mess that you have left
On table, floor and chairs.'

'Untidy Hazel', well, that's what he said,
My teachers felt that way too,
My report always read
'Could do better
If she wasn't a featherhead'.

And then I started out to work
And my boss would say 'keep tidy',
I might obey to what he'd say
But not from Monday till Friday.

And then I started to look at boys,
My dad said, 'That's a laugh,
He'll take one look and sling his hook,
He won't ask for your photograph.'

Then I met a chap, his name was Jack
And he took one look at me,
'She's the girl that I adore
And will marry eventually.'

My dad said, 'Good grief, he's got some nerve
To take on our Hazel's ways,
I'll give him a week to stay the course,
Perhaps I'll stretch to ten days.'

But as you see, he's stood the course
For over fifty years,
The ups and downs, the test of time,
A lot more smiles than tears.

And now my dad's looking down on us
He says, 'By that Jack's a good un
He's looked after my gal all these years,
He wants a putty medal.'

Hazel Palmer

Freedom

Weren't we the lucky ones?
Childhood days were full of fun
Freedom to play in the great outdoors
Freedom to make sandcastles on the shores
Freedom to run down the country lanes
Freedom to pick lovely bluebells again
Freedom to guddle minnows in the burn
Freedom to walk the streets without harm
Childhood days, full of fun
Weren't we the lucky ones?

M S Bradley

When I Was A Kid

When I was a kid, seems a long time ago
The weather knew just what to do
Winter snow, crisp and deep
Snowmen that stayed for weeks and weeks
Sock on hands as well as feet, gloves a luxury yet to meet
Red rings round legs from wellie boots
Corned beef thighs from fires bright
Central heating never known
In mad March the winds blew and in April it showered
Easter we ate and praised the Lord
Whatever happened to Whitsuntide?
Smart new clothes and pennies bright
June promised fluffy white clouds and bluer skies
Sultry days we're longing for
Two weeks away at seaside bay
Never a raindrop to spoil our play
Endless adventures every day
Scabby knees and golden brown arms
Plastic sandals, we had no qualms
No fancy trainers that cost the earth
September song, a new term beckoned
All lined up, let's bang the gong
Autumn play meant conkers soaked in vinegar
An old bootlace for the string, didn't cost a single thing
Dad's old gear suited our guy
Firework rockets lit up the night sky
Nights crept in, the clocks fell back
Twinkling lights began to cheer
Frosty the snowman was soon to appear
Many moons ago when I was a kid
The weather knew just what to do.

Jacqueline Ibbitson

Childhood Home

I stood in a grip of ice
That froze and tossed these old walls
In a tumble of time.
This now-roofless shell,
Which once cradled my
Incipient warmth,
Wrapped my formative years
In a strong embrace
Of sun-stretched days,
And moon-mingled nights
Where quick cats darted through
The garden's sleeping flowers.

Magical summers sang
Their high notes
Through crowded raspberry canes,
And blown poppies blushed
Where dancing emerald blades of grass,
Tickled my freshly formed feet
In whispers of fluting air.

Glancing on my early bed,
A lone bright star
Set in window glass
Shone faintly on my face,
As I painted mind pictures
From wallpaper patterns,
And watched
Faraway house lights
Ripple with curtained thoughts.

Crackling, smoky, autumn fires:
Sledges sliding lamplit tracks
In the cream of winter snows,
Curl back on a tide of years
To soak the cold, empty shell
In happy life once more;
And this sudden rush of memory
Brings my singing childhood home.

David Austin

Wet Work

(For my mother who toiled in pre-machine days)

Monday wash day
Early start morning
Brick copper full of pail
Carried water.

Monday wash day
Wood faggots glowing
Brightly red, steaming
Heated water.

Monday wash day
Scrubbing board standing
Waist-deep in sudsy water
Fingers raw.

Monday wash day
Soapy-smelling air
Blue-bagged rinsing, water
Puddled floor.

Monday wash day
Coloured wintor grey
Cold damp clothes round the
Fire lying.

Monday wash day
Coloured summer gold
With sun-warmed breezes
Easy drying.

Monday wash day
Childhood memories
Hard work and wetness.

An adventure
Which my Hotpoint
Will never allow me . . .
Hopefully.

Ann Edwards

The Good Old Days

When I was young, times were hard
Not easy for the working class,
The men worked hard from dawn to dusk
To bring his family an edible crust.

A scrubbing board, a bar of soap,
An old tin bath to wash the clothes,
A woman's work was never done
To wash the clothes of everyone.

To feed and care for her family brood
She even went without her food,
No finery that she so deserved
And hardly ever a disgruntled word.

Yet through the good times and the bad
Friendships remained with Mum and Dad
And people next door would often drop in
For a laugh and joke or a good old 'chin'.

Remember today if you make a friend
Remain as such till life's end,
Be it as lover, husband or wife,
In good times or bad, in trouble and strife!

W E Clements

The Early Eighties

Would it be good to remember
How London was?
The early eighties, a time of intellectual ferment
When movements now in flower were spawned
Where all developed a consciousness of what was needed

When jobs were rare
And many lived
On the dole
And we lived in the Third World
Among decaying walls and ceilings
And long times waiting for doctors
(That has not changed!)
We lived without money then
As easily as we live with money now

When all the world was potential
And life somehow flourished
Without money
Where materialism
Was a dirty word
What we could not have
We did not want
And vast potential beckoned
That one day things would be better
Or if they were not
That was the way of the world
So we contented ourselves
And thought of ways we could eke out our money a little more
And treasured friendship
A little more.

Alasdair Sclater

People And Places

I remember the lake
And the country lanes
All of the people
And all of their names
The noisy music
We used to play
The friends who died
And went away
I remember the cars
And the journeys we made
The love that was promised
And the plans that were laid
But nothing works out
Like you want it to
What went wrong between us two?
I know I can't turn back the past
But there's something about loving
That makes it last
Maybe the person
Or maybe the place
Whichever it is, 'I have to face'.

Alan Dennis

Forgotten Dreams

My marriage unhappy from the start
The head should have ruled, not my heart.
Within six months, my life turned inside out
We were very different, without a doubt.
A child was on the way
With my mistake I had to stay.
My husband did not communicate
His silences I began to hate.
Children I had two
I really did not know what to do.
Then a third child was born.
And with a situation, I was torn.
He had learning difficulties from the start.
Tore me to pieces, broke my heart.
I carried on in this unwanted match.
All sorts of schemes I tried to hatch.
Then a man came into my life,
Thought I could end this bitter strife.
He became more than just a friend,
This passion I felt could never end.
Everything seemed so right,
The darkness turned into light.
But children have to come first.
Especially the child who came off the worst.
We had to part, it was a sin.
The future seemed so very grim.
I felt my life had been wasted,
A happy relationship I had tasted.
But after a marriage of fifty-six years
I have no time for might-have-been tears.
Five fine grandchildren for my lot.
Perhaps I was right to stay to the end,
But I would like someone to be more than a friend.

Olive Young

Friendship-Days

I sat there alone
Alone as could be
When something
Wonderful happened to me.

He was standing
And knocking upon my door
My special birthday
Had come round once more.

It doesn't seem right somehow
All those years past
Our friendship, our happiness
Laughter and tears
Heartache which lasted these bygone years.

Joy - celebrations
Holidays - fresh - air - sea
Special days, lunch with punch
If we were free.

Shopping - housework
Everything to be done
Most days though - we always had fun.

TV - CDs, our evenings we shared
Togetherness our word
But silence is golden
My memories precious, fading
Away in dreams, now it would seem.

Gail Rowan

Unwillingly To School

No pupils came to school by bus
No parents at the gate.
We knew that there'd be trouble
Were we caught arriving late.

On wooden bench, in silent rows,
We puzzled over fractions,
Why called 'vulgar' - no one knew,
They drove us to distraction.

On special days the parson came
To test how much we knew
Of miracles and holy men
And prophets, brave and true.

Sometimes girls would knit and sew
Days of nerves a-jangling,
Of needle-pricks and stitches dropped
And skeins of wool entangling.

Inkwells filled with chalky ink,
Pen-nibs crossed and broken,
Blots on a page could earn a slap
And sharp words would be spoken.

When people claim that days at school
Were happy times - so carefree -
I just say, 'I beg to differ
And can't possibly agree!'

Joan Brocklehurst

Lostalgia

Oh how people were so much happier then,
To be excited and appreciative of hand-me-downs,
And feel content with their lot,
Not discontented by what they haven't got,
When they would laugh at their own circumstances
And not the circumstances of others,
When buying a new record would keep track of their memories
And not be forgotten once bought,
When television was a novelty rather than a commodity,
Something to switch on when there was a programme to watch,
Not something to switch off when there isn't,
When it was something of communal interest
Not something of individual monotony,
Where queues queued all down the street
For movies that were something to see and not be seen
And people used to eat popcorn until they were sick and not
                                    be sick of popcorn,
Back when the sun shone so much brighter on much
                                    longer afternoons.
Things may seem better now
Though they're not,
We're like spoilt children, not appreciating anything,
Not getting enthusiastic about anything anymore,
Where the get-up-and-go has become the get it and go
Where having everything we want has left us wanting nothing at all.

Anthony Ward

The Thirties, The Loss

My dad, a good man did the best he was able
On pay-day he laid down is pay on the table
Two pound notes it was, to be handled with care
Many mouths to be fed, but we all got a share
My mother was clearing the dishes away
Hard-working she was, very tired, very grey
She picked up the cloth to throw crumbs in the grate
Cried, 'What have I done?' but her cry was too late
Two pound notes were burnt, all the money we had
Our straits became desperate, in times that were bad
My mother was crying, my father went pale
The little ones frightened, they started to wail
My mother, dejected, looked down at her brood,
'Just how will we live, with no money for food?'
The few things we had, they all went into 'hock'
My father's good suit and a wedding gift clock
It took many months to get over the loss
But my poor dear mum, ever carried that cross.

Gordon Andrews

Smelly Memories

In Stokes' Coffee House I dwell
When I smell that coffee smell
The smell of coffee wafting all around
As we shopped around the town.

When I smell bacon on the breeze
I'm wafted back with greatest ease
To the grocer's years ago
The bacon slicer on the go.

The smell of butter takes me back
To watch patterns forming on the pat
See it then expertly wrapped
The ladies all had quite a knack.

When it's lavender I smell
I smell the hedge where I did dwell
When smell of tar comes to me
A steamroller is what I see.

When creosote assails my sense
I see Dad putting it on the fence
When I smell the smell of chalk
Again I hear my teacher talk.

To smell the grass now I know
Takes me to fields I played in long ago.
To smell the smells of memory
Is so very dear to me.

Stroma Hammond

Friendship

Best of friends for 40 years
Through good times and bad
We lived by different time clocks
Our tastes in every way
Were completely different
What we wore, what we ate
Our attitude to life
As opposite as could be
No agreements on policy
Of any political group
Arguing interminably
When all we shared was hope
Yet through many turbulent years
We stayed close and shared
Our fundamental values
At roots we were inseparable
At heart we really cared.

B Williams

Finnishing School

From school bells to church bells
To sleigh bells for wedding bells

We met first in form five and were together
For a whole five years
A fat snotty-nosed friend but one to rely on
For help with spelling - to share sweets
And marbles - but not hankies
We went our separate ways in form eleven
Though we promised to write - we never did
By then he was as fat as a barrel - spotty but brainy
Into bikes, but with all his faults - he was my hero
I'd once heard he'd left and went to college then uni
I'd left and gone into office life - now off to Norway
Exploring the streets and squares - I wandered
Enjoying the break - and the clean crisp air
Someone shouted - Anna - everyone, including me, turned
To see a tall, academic, well-groomed man - coming towards me
I smiled and shouted hello - to my surprise
It was my snotty-nosed, spotty hero - Henry - from long ago
We clung on like there's no tomorrow and never been apart
Now both twenty-eight - free and single - partners once had
Are no more - we talked and laughed for hours
A promise made and kept by that Christmas
We returned as two and left as one - by sleigh bells.
Class dismissed.

David Charles

Yorkshire Mist (Missed)

Rolling hills, meadows and streams
Drystone walls that map out the seams

Breathtaking landscapes, mist on the moor
Walking through heather that blankets the floor

Old cobbled streets and steep hills they climb
Stopping to rest as church bells chime

Steam train whistles as it rounds the hills
Passing sleepy villages and long-forgotten mills

A quaint country pub to rest for a while
The view from the window conjures a smile

Lost in its beauty you can't help but find
Yorkshire is forever in your heard and mind.

Gail Goree

Shadows Of Dreams

Take a stroll down memory lane
To live again
That 'yesteryear'
When happiness was all
And I took it for granted
I couldn't see the wealth
I had in someone
Yes, some like you
I had the world
When we were together
So faithful and true
But I didn't see
The warning light
Until it was too late
We drifted apart
No last goodbyes
Just broken dreams
And a broken heart.

Margaret Parnell

Old Shoes

I have made with sadness a decision today
That is to throw an old pair of shoes away
Shoes that have taken me many a place
Sometimes at a crawl, sometimes at a pace.

Together we've been to town and back
Over hills and fields carrying a rucksack
We've visited family and friends
Missed buses and had to walk a road's end.

Together we've been soaked by rain
Battled against gales and hurricane
We've slipped and slithered on ice and snow
In fog got lost not knowing which way to go.

We've been together through good and bad
Times that's been happy and also sad
You took me to see my grandchildren born
Helped them take first steps across the lawn.

You were there when I won at darts
Wo paced together as my marriage fell apart
I've covered you in tears when cause to weep
When my mum and dad took their final sleep.

With memories happy and sad I shed a tear
As I say goodbye to a pair of friends
That I hold so dear.

James Friday

A Walk Down Memory Lane

The Royal Navy was a way of life
In the 50s there was no strife
There were few comforts at sea or ashore
Discipline was tough right to the core
Of ships and barracks where men were messed
Conditions were basic and not always best
Yes, there were moans and grumbling too
Not like now where 'I'll sue, sue, sue!'
You did the job for which you'd trained
Muttered and grumbled and complained
Only to your mate would you utter thought
But not too loud - for you may be caught . . .
So you did your job in rain or sun
'Stow that gear; clean that gun'
'Get up the mast, paint the yards'
'Clean your rifle for tomorrow's guards'
'Clear lower deck for divisions'
Or captain's defaulters for decisions
Routines were tight and rightly so
(You didn't argue with the PO)
Who passed the orders down the line
We obeyed and did not whine
For one day we could climb
To the heights of rank where we'd direct
And fellow shipmates we'd inspect
As on deck we would all fall-in
Standing proud with jutting chin
As our ship entered harbour with pennants tight
For a ship fully dressed is a wonderful sight
Even after time far over the sea
To come back to England meant a lot to me
So looking back at those times long ago
I've feelings of nostalgia, today's young will never know!

Alan R Coughlin

A Time Of Innocence

Let me take you to a time
That I know so very well
Like a favourite nursery rhyme
It weaves a magic spell.

The days seemed to last a lifetime
As we wandered country roads
Adventures took us far and wide
Everything gleamed like gold.

You could still have doors unlocked
When you went down to the pub
Or if you nipped down to the shops
You had no fear of being mugged.

Lost in nineteen fifty-three
Those happy days stand proud
Unrestricted and so carefree
A time of innocence - sang out loud.

Frank Howarth-Hynes

The Good Old Days

Was it so good in the 'Good Old Days'?
You were always having to scrimp and scrape
And if you were lucky to have an apple
Goodness me, what a treat,
You'd eat it going down the street
If you had false teeth then, it was a real big grapple
Oh! What a lovely taste they had
Then you would think things weren't really that bad.

You would call on a lady to do the lot
She'd deliver the babies or else laid them out,
And if you were posh and you had a jug and bowl
You could lend it out without a scowl,
'Cause not everyone had one of these
Nor did they have many clothes,
And perhaps they'd borrow a couple of bob
You'd lend it them till they got a job.

Everything was on food ration
No wonder there was a lot of passion
They had really large families then
But folks would always rally round, and
No cars, lots of bikes
You either walked or hitch-hiked
There's not much choice at all
But you saved yourself from falling to the wall.

And when you sat down at night if you were able
You'd put the wireless on the table
Wilfred Pickles would say, 'Give her the money Mabel.'
Go to the flicks and watch Betty Grable
'In the Good Old Days'.

There was no TV to sit and watch
But you could leave your door on the latch
But people would rally round
If they found you hadn't a pound
'Cause it saved you going to the old pawn shop,
You may have pawned your wedding ring
That wasn't a very good thing,
It spent more time in that shop
Than it did on the women's third finger
Outside the shop you would then linger
Wondering if you could get it back
Back in the good old days.

The bathroom then was called the 'lav'
'Twas outside in the freezing cold
You had to pluck up the courage, you felt quite bold
You never had toilet rolls
You sat and froze in the good old days
And before and after the war, when you think back
You were really quite poor
Back in the good old days.

I know which I'd sooner have.

Sheila Moore

No U-Turn

I remember the days when I washed with a dolly
A sort of cow's udder on the end of a pole -
Then came the twin-tub, which on the whole
Was better, though messy not exceedingly jolly.
Vegetables muddy, no vacuum-packed meat
You tasted the cheese, sugar was weighed.

Without animal rights, game was proudly displayed
And the now cheap chicken, a special treat
Shopping was a sociable day
There was only the seasonal choice
Each small retailer had distinctive voice
Not megastore's present bewildering display
There was need to preserve every crop
Salted and bottled, smoked the odd ham
Summer to autumn we'd never stop.
We soaked and washed every nappy
No spray polish, just elbow grease
Lots of ironing, all clothes crease
In evenings the wireless to keep us happy
Now the young are reverting to be green
Some of the old ways are back again
With all of that effort, all of that strain . . .
No thanks, I'll continue my new easy scene!

D Bagshawe

Looking Back

I remember a time when I walked down the street
And nasty gum didn't stick to my feet

I remember a time not so long ago
When one heard of a friend having polio

I remember a time when I was young
And round the piano duets would be sung

In Paris I hear the pavements are cleaner
But political fights are also keener

Now polio is a thing of the past
But TB is returning fast

Still piano playing does exist
But keyboard players are hard to resist

In schools and hospitals all around
New initiatives are being found

To keep us in the pink of health
And the league tables creeping up by stealth

For most of us life is better now
But looking back befits us somehow

Memory is a precious thing
And better by far than lots of bling!

Barbara Tozer

One Year Of Jonathan

I never cried for you, Jonathan
Or myself when we took our last ride
Ice in the heart and a shattered faith
Was all that was left when you died.
I locked up the room with the gaping crib
And the teddy bear's glass-eyed stare
Resenting the mocking reminders
That you had been theirs to share.
The days became weeks, the weeks grew to months
That stretched to a stillborn decade
While seasons changed unnoticed
And music was left unplayed
Then fate took a hand, the day I unearthed
Your long-lost, very first shoe
Soft and diminutive, hardly worn
With a pompom of fuzzy blue.

When the floodgates opened at last I found
The release that comes with mourning
As bluebells gave me back your eyes
And your smile in the day's bright dawning.
Rose petals told of your tender cheeks
And I felt the warmth of the sun
As the barren years dissolved, in recalling
The joy you had brought me in one.

Dorothy Kellett

King Coal Is Dead, Long Live The King

Looking back, there was something incredibly secretive
About the pit, a workplace shrouded in mystery
Where only grown-ups ever went, particularly the men,
And which seemed to make them tired, so depleted
Of energy when they returned at the end of the day
To recuperate, before leaving to begin all over again.

It was what the old, apparently, had once done,
And which they frequently reflected upon, at length,
As if addicted to the retelling of experiences so trying,
So debilitating, that their effects still lingered on,
In faces etched by strain and bodies robbed of strength,
Yet holding on, like shadows in light that is dying.

But that won't be a legacy for my generation,
The first to break free of the mining work mould
By choice, and to train for a healthier job instead,
For those dark days of coal have almost gone,
Collieries will soon close and their prime land sold,
As nuclear power lights the new cleaner way ahead.

Andrew Farmer

Days Gone By

When I was a child
The sun always shone
Now there are no values
And love has gone.

No respect for parents
Children run wild
How things have changed
Since I was a child.

We had a loving firm hand
To teach us what's right
Now it's the gangs
That roam the night.

Oh, how I wish
For times gone by
As I look at youngsters
With a sad sigh.

Julie Brown

Street Song

They called it Carlyle Street, no one knew why.
Some thought it was the name of town up north
or just a bloke who was given the land
for holding some dead king's flag in battle.
But it wasn't.

It ran as straight as a sheet of rolled steel,
all along one side of the steelworks wall.
Some said that it was built by the Romans
but they wouldn't build such a street as that
would they?

A row of houses stood facing the wall.
One up, one down and back to back, and when
the rent man called we locked our doors and hid
until he roared, 'I'll have you all next week.'
But he didn't.

At night we lay awake, four in one bed
and heard, next door, through walls worn whisper-thin
their muffled laughter and cries of delight.
My brother said that they were saying prayers.
But they weren't.

When war began they tried to bomb the works,
but missed and blew up the houses instead.
A mother, five kids and their gran - all dead.
Their dad should have come back from the army.
But he never.

They packed us off to where there was nothing
to fear, but ferocious cows in fields and
a raucous cock that woke us every day
at dawn. We wished a bomb would drop on him
But it didn't.

I have never gone back, but they tell me
the works, the wall and houses have all made way
for bistros and bingo and all-night clubs
where men strip off to entertain women.
But that can't be. Can it?

John Eccles

The Patchwork Quilt

She sat alone in the firelight glow
This little old lady of long ago
Beside her, her faithful tabby cat lay
Her constant companion day by day
Gently she rocked in her old oak chair
Softly she hummed to herself sitting there
As she worked with her needle and bright coloured thread
Making a beautiful patchwork bedspread.

Each square held a memory, to her very dear
Of things that had happened in her yesteryear
Here a small piece from a dress that she wore
At a party she went to aged just twenty-four
It was there that she met the love of her life
Becoming his sweetheart and then his dear wife
Here is a piece from her trousseau and this
Comes from her first baby's gown, oh what bliss!

There are squares from school uniforms, an apron or two
Check shirts of her husband's and curtains of blue
A piece from a ballgown brings memories to treasure
Each stitch she puts in gives her so much pleasure
Her hands may be gnarled and dimmed be her sight
But she hummed as she worked, well into the night
And she rocked in her chair in the firelit room
Steadily working on the patchwork heirloom.

Barbara Dunning

Blinded By Sunlight

I dreamed again last night *(she graciously said)*;
    Of ships that sailed;
Of meadows green; and willow trees that swayed;
Of buttercups in the breeze
And bluebells shielded from too much sunlight.

I'll dream again tonight
In vivid colours as before
    Of things past
When you and I breathed in fresh air
Sampled nature
Never thinking it would impair.

I'll dream of your happy face
That used to be
The grand-times we had
Frolicking in the gentle sea:

Such a long time ago. Yet it never fades - the memories linger -
Waiting to be replayed:

She sighs a sad sigh: and clutches my arm rising from her invalid chair
Her gnarled fingers grasping hold of the white stick,
She now has to take with her everywhere . . .

Alan Knott

Places

They are forever here
in the landscape of my mind.
'There are places I'll remember all my life
though some have gone', the song goes.

But these will never go:

Scottish borders -
Carterhatch, its sloping sunlit fields
enfolding vales, eternal in the sunlight
of that first fine summer;
Spooky Woods and Smelly Corner
christened by spellbound kids.

Green Farm deep in Herefordshire:
across the road we
wander in shining apple orchards;
on warm nights spy quicksilver bats
and burrowing badgers.

Mighty, mythical Cornwall -
the sand-dune land of Praa Sands;
Polperro's toytown streets;
timeless space of Looe estuary.

Such places hold my heart in thrall,
like loved ones dear to me - yet not,
for places never die, nor do their memories.

Wes Ashwell

The Man From Long Ago

The look in his eyes was wistful
His smile was faint, but there
In the faded photograph
She had kept in a frame with care
Who was he? everyone wondered
That man from long ago
Whose memory she so cherished
That she kept his picture on show
She sits in the old armchair now
Her eyes not seeming to see
But if she looks at his image
Then all who watch agree
She seems like she remembers
And her face is all aglow
Whenever she gazes upon
The man from long ago.

Jackie Painter

I Remember

I remember, I remember, leaving home to start anew
Getting a job, living out, was something I had to do.
So to Chailey Heritage, Sussex, I went to nurse the children there
(The first day, I remember, me falling off a chair).
I loved it working in that place, with children everywhere
The polio and the TB kids were nursed out in the air.

I was just sixteen when I went to work with little kids so small
My friends were just as young as me - some short and others tall.
I learned a great deal working there - 'twas two short years or so
And then to Southlands' Hospital, Shoreham - real nursing I would go.

In training school we studied the body and the mind
Went up on to the wards each day to see what we would find.
When on the ward with tiny tots, I loved the Sister there
She was so marvellous with those kids - she taught me how to care.
Then much to my amazement, she awarded me a prize
That year, I was the best ward nurse - I couldn't believe my eyes!

As I went round the other wards, learning all the way
Trained nurse to be my chosen path ('twas very low the pay).
But, working really hard I did to further my career
I took exams and studied well and shed a happy tear.
The great day came, I finally got that magic badge to say -
'A Registered Nurse at last you are', 'twas such a happy day!

Helen Sarfas

Thoughts

I've been told our days are numbered
And that we shall part
Knowing this upsets me
The idea breaks my heart.

We've been together many years
Not always for the best
All I know for sure
Is our love has passed the test.

In the past we both made plans
But went our separate ways
Now we live together
And share the hours of every day.

I just can't imagine
How my life will be
When I'm left here on my own
With just my memories.

When my life is over
One thing is very plain
Wait for me in Heaven
And we'll be together once again.

Farina Jenkins

Childhood Memories

It seems like only yesterday
We left old England's shore
And I can still remember well
The years that went before.

In my childhood memories
The earth seems fresh and clean
The crispness after falling snow
Glistening hedgerows, pastures green.

Gathering bluebells in the backwood
Buttercups in the spring
Playing happily round the old mill
Hearing robins sing.

I remember winter evenings
Snowflakes falling, twilight's charm
Family gatherings round the fireside
Roasting chestnuts, keeping warm.

These memories of England
Though many years have passed
Are held so tightly in my heart
Where all good memories last.

Doreen Mezzomo

My Grandma

I remember so vividly
Visiting Grandma when I was small
She lived in the next village
How we got there I can't recall
Such things as buses were not for us
So suppose we had to walk
Eating up the miles so fast
As we laughed and talked
Grandma was a little lady
With long skirts to the floor
And the cleanest whitest apron
Even though she was poor
Out in her back garden stood an apple tree
Grandpa hung a swing for us children
To swing from happily
At the bottom of the garden ran a railway track
Taking all its passengers
From here to there and back
It was a huge great monster
Billowing smoke all the way
Sending out little dots of soot
Making everything dirty and grey
The whistle from the engine
Could be heard from many miles away
And I stood there at the fence to watch
The excitement of the day
Just before Mum took me home
Grandma changed her boots
And I sat on the hassock
Doing up the buttons with a hook
Now I am old with grandchildren and great-grandchildren
And as I sit and reminisce
The shrill of the telephone disturbs me
It's one of my own with a goodnight kiss.

Daphne Fryer

Memories, Memories, Memories

Asked to test one's memory,
Going back seventy or eighty years
And recall childhood activity,
Without too many fears.

It was a different world,
Since then so much has unfurled,
Is it better or is it worse
Or is it just another curse?

Let's think back when a child,
When recollections can be intense,
Home life so much more mild,
When life evolved round pence.

In those days TV known only to a few,
Alexandra Palace to the fore,
Just one thing now taken on cue,
There has been so much more.

Even electricity not known to many,
Candles and gas, to see the light,
Solid fuel ovens the only heat, if any,
Old-fashioned kettles, black not bright.

Fridges and freezers not even seen,
Nor were telephones, let alone mobiles,
Public phone box only on stream,
While bathrooms were few down the aisles.

A brick-clad copper met those needs,
Galvanised iron bath completed the deeds,
Once a week, on a Friday night,
Proving such a regular delight.

Washing machines and clothes dryers
Manual workers instead, the doers,
Lavatories accessed from outside,
Too cold to sit out on the side.

Our friends we met outside
And there our pleasures applied,
All sorts of games were involved,
On the spot problems quickly resolved.

Very scarce being the traffic,
Football on the road was classic,
Then, of course, there was cricket,
With a gas lamp post as the wicket.

Cowboys and Indians, guns that went pop,
A local policeman might cause us to stop,
But with hopscotch on the pavement,
Such games there our intent.

Cigarette cards, we used to flick,
Hop, skip and jump came into the trick,
Alleys and marbles rolling along,
We knew the street in which we did belong.

Conkers too in the autumn time,
Finding the toughest with which to shine,
Chalk pictures on the pavement,
Silly rhymes chanted, we did not resent.

These games too were played at school,
Different friends, but a similar tool,
Then there was the scouts,
Two evenings when we were out.

Weekends took on another role
Most Saturdays, the allotment filled the scroll,
With Sunday school the next day,
In the evening, the choir to play.

Later, after being employed,
A bicycle purchased, really enjoyed,
Riding out with friends,
New countryside, breaking new trends.

Takeaways confined to chips,
With fish to add if you could afford the bits,
For cod and chips, tuppenny and a pennerf,
Thankfully received, it really was worth.

Pizzas and burgers not then in the trend,
American influence was still round the bend,
For the older ones, a bottle of beer,
Was really something they could soundly cheer.

Memories come flooding back,
Too many making up the pack.
Anything achieved needed work,
There was no time then to shirk.

As we said, a different world.

George Beckford

Champion Baylands Sparky

Sparky was dark and sweet of eye
Sparky, a collie, a beautiful tri
Sparky matured like fine summer wine
Sparky was quite well known in his time.

He and I were once a pair
Travelling to shows without a care
Mostly by rail, it was better then
What's that you say? You wish to know when?

Sparky grew older, a little more mellow
Sparky grew rounder, a portly old fellow
Sparky gave pleasure in so many ways
Sparky came to the end of his days.

Flora Denning

To Honey - Our Dog

Farewell dear friend
Closed are those liquid eyes
That steadfast gaze on mine.
Stilled is the tail
That waved with eager joy
At my approach.
That questing nose -
Forever so it seems -
Scrutinising blade and leaf
Along the hedge and bank
Snuffs no more.
Your gentle velvet head
Rests no more upon entwined
Thrusting paws,
Nor pressing heavy upon my knee
Awaiting some move, some sign
Of impending walks.

Merle Chacksfield

Back To My Roots

On a trip down memory lane,
I looked around in the drizzling rain
At places that were part of life
For me before and since, a wife.

I walked the streets I knew so well,
The place of work - that's where I fell
In love. That man I long since married,
His children I've lovingly carried.

The shops have changed where, once, I bought
The goods that, then, cost next to nought.
The people too, seem different now -
I'm sure, before, they weren't so loud.

Perhaps it's me who's changed. I'm older,
Not quite so shy, in fact much bolder.
'Would you return?' I'm often asked
Well, no; for me what's passed is past.

Maureen Steele

Lazy Afternoons

Sunshine fills the room,
As I wait for you.
The day has only just begun,
For soon you will come to me.
When I see you walk into the room,
My heart begins to pound.
You smile at me with flashing eyes,
Promises of fantasies come true.
The touch of your hands, so gentle and so soft,
Stir feelings of forgotten words, love and lust;
Begin to fill my soul.
Memories of endless nights and
Days full of laughter and joy.
Of walks barefoot on the sand
Or climbing rocks, so rugged and rough.
The future comes into view,
Endless nights alone with you.
Holidays full of crystal-blue seas,
Dolphins swimming and the summer breeze.
Your lips touch mine, just in time,
Breaking my thoughts; you shatter my mind.
Passion then starts to stir
As your kisses unlock the girl.

A M Williamson

Jogging The Memory

Just been travelling on a steam train
Childhood memories came flooding back
Seeing the coal going into the engine
Watching the men repairing the track.
The smell of steam in my nostrils
Is something, I can honestly say
I've always fondly remembered
And so much enjoy to this day.
Chugging along at an easy pace
Looking around at the countryside
Listening to the noise of the engine
Thoroughly enjoying the ride.
As a child in Grandma's garden
I used to stand and watch the train
Wondering where folk were going
And when they would be back again?
They would often smile and wave at me
I would wave back with all my might
Until the train turned the corner
And was no longer in my sight.
Isn't it funny as we grow older
We start thinking of days long past?
Some things are so easily forgotten
Whilst other memories seem to last.

Judith Watts

Rustic

Desert sands
There he stood
Fifteen hands,
Army stable, his home
With me, he would roam.
A canter, a gallop or trot
On patrol, weather hot
Early morn with a neigh
He thanked me
For his morning hay,
I cleaned his room
His servant, an RMP
Lance Corporal groom,
The time 2am
Up to the hills of
'Jerusalem'.
Clippety-clop
Clippety-clop
Street lights, jumping shadows
Over the top,
Come nineteen forty-eight
Sadly I had to say goodbye
Stable gates, tears in my eye,
My mate 'Rustic'
From the Barbary Coast,
A flea-bitten grey.
Are you forgotten
Neigh lad, neigh!

Frank Baggaley

Old Flames

From the beginning
Beautiful
Nights were numerous

Passionate days spent
On
The brink of agony

Later we met in a
Small
Café by the sea

Hesitantly we picked
Up
The lost threads
Dipped
Biscuits in our tea

We rambled on through
Sundry
Flotsam and old memories

Tide swept seaweed on
The
Shoreline, tangled up
Like
Old discarded tights

Although discreet the
Past
Is always present.

Rupert Smith

Country Reared

In the country we were reared my brother and I
In a cottage down a long winding lane
Our family didn't have much money then
But we always got by
Family values we were taught right from the very start
Good manners and discipline were known from the heart
Dad went out to work early to earn our daily bread
And Mum looked after us kids and the home
And worked part-time instead
Mum was always there to see us off to school
And met us off the bus in the afternoon as a rule
We had a coal fire for which we had to chop sticks
To keep us warm at night
And we both had a hot-water bottle that we'd take to bed
Porridge and toast for breakfast and always a cooked tea
There would be to keep us healthy and germ-free
Board games we would play on the floor by the fire
And colouring books were aplenty for our desire
Dad would come home and we'd all sit at the table for tea
Then we'd watch TV, then it would be baths and to bed
And a story we'd be read
Each day was a surprise, we'd play marbles and hopscotch outside
Or ride our bikes through filth and mud
Weekends we'd have pocket money if our chores had been done
Then down to the corner shop we would run
A comic and sweets would be a treat
Then we'd find a quiet seat to sit and eat
A den we would build out of square hay bales in the field
We'd hide-and-seek to our hearts' content
And simple games we would invent
Conkers and hedge nuts we would collect
Blackberries and mushrooms were plentiful too
Damsons, apples and plums we'd collect for a pie
From starvation we would never die
We had many a visitor come to our house down the long country lane
A milkman, a paperboy and a coalman too
An electric meter man in his van to empty the tin
That Mum had to put her shillings in

Dad would take us for walks in the woods
And we'd watch the birds building their nests
And collect bluebells to take home in our vests
Tadpoling we would go with our butterfly nets in tow
But rarely did we have much to show
In the country we were reared, my brother and I.

Jane Horton

Last Train To Camelford

I will no more a-roving to Camelford by train
Experiencing 'Ns' and 'Us' steaming in the rain
Bringing Cornwall nearer on the Withered Arm
(Even Halwill Junction had a certain charm).

Oh, a lengthy journey from London Waterloo
(Attaching destinations was then the thing to do)
Arriving very weary - hungry - late at night
Vanished were the taxis - completely out of sight.

Now seasoned tourists travel by their car
Clogging lanes in summer - Padstow down to Par
Ah but a memory - some forty years ago
Last train to Camelford - such a bitter blow.

Steve Glason

Late January Outside Scunthorpe Museum 1970

Aconites permeate the ground
In bunches and early frost
Gradually melting in satin crusts.

The museum sparkles in the sunshine
And the hum of traffic waxes and wanes
Snowdrops mingle with doves' droppings
And the church's mellow bricks look
Like old cheese in the low morning sun.

Mosaic paving stones, spiky grass and
The intermittent piercing sparrow song
Seems to weave peace
And to scream it.

Endless faces in a crowd on a wet day
And glossy pavements reflecting tired faces
Reflecting tired monuments.
Tall spiky figures and traffic police
Manipulate the car - people's stares,
Gritty and misunderstanding.

Small children going to school cheer them
Among the wet slimy leaves,
Above, starlings encircling the trees around
In clouds dropping like rain on the grounds and
Late winter month's clouds frown in an uncontentious way.

The stark little snowdrops piercing through the brown,
Endless grasses near the church nearby seem to
Leadenly rage against the stones, like
A medieval symphony, the hours are
Publishing history here.
Dogs sniffing, smiling and moving on -
Children wide-mouthed and innocent moving on
Past ceaselessly, this building of a hundred years.

Doreen Sylvester

Midnight In Moscow

I realised my dream one night
Under Moscow skies.
I stood beneath the Kremlin walls
Where Russia's true heart lies.

The rich red ramparts stood aloft
As testaments to time
And stately towers overlooked
The citadel sublime.

Night cast its shadows dark and deep
Over Lenin's tomb
And ghosts of buried heroes walked
In hallowed halls of gloom.

Visions of glory raised their domes
Like eastern turbans fashioned
Painted in gold by artisans
With love of art impassioned.

Like shapes of candy topped with whirls
St Basil's seemed to me -
A miracle of God-like skill
And chiselled poetry.

Buildings of beauty, subtly lit,
Revealed their awesome splendour.
Enchantment held me in its spell
And filled the air with wonder.

Impressions dimmed by time can fade
But feelings will endure
And moments rare and beautiful
The years will not obscure.

Celia Thomas

Better In The Sixties

When I compare my daughters' lives
To the quiet life I led;
As wife and mum in the sixties
It really has to be said.

I consider my life was better
The simple life I knew;
Just bringing up our children
Being there for my husband too.

Our daughters today both go to work
They have to, every day,
There's the high cost of a mortgage
Plus other bills to pay.

When I was young in the sixties
You never heard of wild road-rage;
No shooting in our city streets
Drunken binges of teenage.

No mobile phones' intrusive tones
Disturbed the quiet air;
Looking round at life today
I feel a sad despair.

Yes, England in the sixties
Was a wonderful place to live;
To go back to those golden days
Oh, what a lot I'd give.

Shirley Brooks

Down Memory Lane

How I remember my childhood
The eldest of my mother's brood
Dad worked just down the road
Mum was a housewife who washed and sewed
Me and my brother played football outside
On a pavement not very wide
I explored the district on my bike
Just a youngster, a little tyke
When Dad came home we sat down to tea
Then we all gathered round the TV
That was us till the light went out
Next morning we had to be up and about
Such was our life a long time ago
How life has changed as we all know.

Frank Tonner

Familiar Stranger

This little box contains
All that I know of you

Its lid inlaid with strips of brass
Still opens to reveal your self

A letter to a dear one speaks
Of hopes and plans that died before your death

But though we never met I find you here
In this brief message from a new-found land

Richard Henry

Way Out West

Some day soon
To head out west again
And stand where I have stood
Upon the Cliffs of Moher;

Or look down
From the summit of Croagh Patrick
Upon the islands studding the azure
Of Clew Bay;

Or watch the sun go down
On Achill Island
Where Slievemore with the sun behind it
Is the shadow of a mountain;

Or frolic like an astronaut
Upon the lunar landscape
That is the limestone pavement
Of the Burren;

Or stand outside
The most westerly pub in Europe
And look from the Dingle Peninsular
Out to the Blaskets.

To head out west
And see and do all that
I will have gone a long way
Beyond the Pale,

Motoring over roads that are a part
Of a filtration process which ensures
That only the very best
Make it to the west.

Stan Downing

A Walk In My Mind

My walk in my mind is in mem'ry
Of childhood days long ago
My life has now reached its September
So I'll try my best to remember
The places I used to know.

I cross the road - hardly need to look
For I seldom see a car -
But there is the milkman with his dray
I hope he'll give me a lift today
Though it won't be very far.

Over the stile in the old stone wall
And then down the other side -
Hooray the farmer is making hay
A lovely place for us to play
In the sheaves where we can hide.

Then through the allotment gardens
That bring back old memories
Men busily digging and weeding
Planting and sowing and seeding
Growing food for their families.

I walk on the path by the quarry
With the ropeworks through the gate
A family of ducks swim on the pool
What a lovely walk to go to school -
Now it's a housing estate.

Doreen Wright

Gone Bye Days

I often dream of days gone by with horse and cart and carriage
Following after with a spade to create a garden barrage.

I often dream of shops gone by, spicy with aromas
Cheeses, butter, soap and hams surrounded by the mouse cud.

I often think of old school rules, the three Rs, strict, unbending
Writing with the flowery loops, pride in all the rendering.

I often dream of the old mill, noisy, dark and draughty
Working all the days God sent, with teacher ever haughty.

I often dream of Ma and Pa, Grandma and Grandpappy
Outings on a seaside spree, rock, donkeys and happy.

I often dream of when we wed, when you returned from war
Our lovely little terraced home that we strived to pay for.

I often dream of our firstborn whose face I can't remember
The stinging tears I still recall, bereavement ever embers.

I often dream of when we met and of the time we parted,
The years of old age never yours, whilst mine are being counted . . .

Melody

I've Known You A Long Time

I've known you a long time
Like tomorrow wasn't there
My heart has been beating like
Nobody else has the right to
Some sunshine and numerous
Summer storms. The sun is shining
With the clouds and the rain
Like kettles have been boiling
A million times a day. I've always
Known you as long as I can think
There were tears around, the kitchen
Sink. I never forgot you like the
Winter wind rustling the trees alive
The sun is always with me like I
Love you still, it always ends the same.
Like tomorrow never comes I've known
You a long time like the shadows of
Countless winter snows. I've known
You a long time, I've known you
A very long time!

David Rosser

The Changing Times

As I walk down my memory lane
I see youngsters skipping - duffel coats
A teacher waiting, wielding cane
Spy crates of milk on horse-drawn floats
Coalman humping a heavy sack
A dustman striding down our path
Anchovy paste in lunch box pack
Postman's sherry - Christmas aftermath!
'Stop me and buy one' a Walls ice cream -
One penny is all that we would need.
Jam made by mother - your senses dream . . .
To taste the fruit was fancy indeed.
Fresh crusty bread brought to the door
And 'Memory Lane' cakes - so enticing
The Old Corner Shop - hub of gossip galore . . .
A walk with a memory is always inviting.

Beryl Mapperley

Days In Alexandrea Park

A rain-drenched Tuesday evening
The pitter-patter of tiny feet
Does not go unnoticed.
Little Miss Craven pushing a pram
Further towards her father's
Disapproval
The duck-diving lakes
Where a lonely lothario takes
A break - are untarnished
By the wind's autumn leaf removal.

A labyrinth of lost treasure
From when pirate adventures
Made Sam walk the plank.
Little Mr Foster kisses a toad;
Making a wish to play
Guitar like Prince.
A high-flying heron receives
A bird's-eye view of chocolate buttons
And muddy sleeves - I wince now
At how much I miss my crew.

Marc E Wright

Sweet Memories

She looks into the mirror
And sees the wrinkles there
Memories drift back of a young girl
With beautiful golden hair

She puts on lots of make-up
To cover creases there
In her mind she sees a young face
With skin so smooth and fair

She gets up from the table
With joints that pain from wear
She once had legs so slender
They made the young men stare

Across the room she ambles
Slowly now, she cannot rush
In her mind she is dancing
A foxtrot, a tango, a waltz

She goes into the garden
Her poodle by her side
Imagining him a stallion
The one she used to ride

Indoors there is an old man
His hair is white as snow
In her eyes he is young and handsome
The boy she used to know.

Doreen Gardner

The Garden In Memory Lane

With teardrops are the flowers watered here,
Their blossoms with no others can compare.
To walk, and muse, in such a place so fair,
Is to be safely rescued from despair.

So, gently back in time we go again
No other can compare these memories sweet,
So freshly fair and all with love complete,
Forever and forever to remain.

So, dry those eyes and set your heart on high,
Knowing those blooms so delicate and rare,
Will last forever, and, at your call, be there
Beyond destruction and all earthly fear.

Mary Hughes

My Village

I wandered through my village - where I was born
And where I spent such a wonderful childhood
And I thought, *What have they done to my home?*

The school and the church on the hill
And the Inn - all belong to the Glebe
What memories of schooldays and Sunday school!
And the lady who cleaned the church - wearing her husband's cap!

Down in the heart of the village, was the Leat
Where we played around and drank from
And there, lived the lady, who was the village 'midwife'
And 'laid out the dead'.

The two brothers lived opposite, who made the coffins
And delivered them on a handcart.
They covered them with a red cloth,
The villagers would stand and stare
As they passed wondering 'for whom?'

I remember the cows walking through the village,
From the fields at 4 o'clock
They knew where to go - it was milking time
And back next morning at 9 o'clock - just as we were off to school.

The lady who delivered the milk from a churn
Always the same greeting, 'Well, it's nice now,'
Or if it was raining, 'Well; it's not so nice now.'
Her curly hair dripping with raindrops.

I remember at harvest time
We gathered in the fields
We played 'hay sweet' and shared their bread and cheese.

On Good Fridays we spent all day
At our allotments - with our fathers,
The day was for 'tilling' and picking primroses
It was always a sunny day - blessed with Easter.

But now it's all gone - we've grown up
And it's re-inhabited by strangers from afar
They'll never know about our wonderful childhoods
For it's all a concrete jungle!

Oh, what have they done to my village?

Betty Prescott

Reminiscence

It's nice to reminisce when I was a lad
Most days were happy, very few sad
Life was hard and wages low
But we were kept healthy and all of aglow

We used to play football safe in the park
From after tea till almost dark
There was a time we had to abide
Else parents would be ready to smack your hide

In summer, skipping ropes across the street
If we saw a car, what a treat
Hopscotch, tig and kick the can
These games were played before my life began

On Christmas Eve we hung our sock
To be filled with an orange, sixpence and a top
No computer games for us or DVD
The ones we had only totalled three

We never complained of nothing to do
Just made things up and saw them through
With very little money to go out
We enjoyed life with almost nowt

Now looking back as a lad
I'm lucky for the life I've had
With plenty of enjoyable years
And only a few that brought tears

They think we are past our sell-by date
For us things were never served on a plate
We are strong and stand up tall
That's why our generation came through the war.

Anthony Griffiths

My Town

My kind of town! Oh yes, my kind of town
It was, but how it has changed.
Westover Road once the Bond Street of Bournemouth.
Now, well what can I say? No words to describe it.
How can anyone understand buildings of great beauty, torn down,
Others of no use taking their place;
One such building voted the second ugliest building in Britain.
Expensive car parks lurk everywhere.
No place to sit and rest on beautiful cliffs, looking out to sea.
At night, the town is no place to be, flashing lights
The children to attract, young people in their teens.
No, at night it's no place to be.
This walk down Memory Lane so very sad to remember how it was
Just ten or so years ago.

Audrey Allen

When Mam Was At Catholic School

When Mam was at Catholic school,
A long time ago,
They had 'plasticine'
And 'not Play-Doh' . . .

They had chalk and slate
Before pencil, paper and ink,
And you 'had to sit still' -
'Hardly moving' to think . . .

Most nun teachers were strict;
And you couldn't complain
Or they'd lash out at you
With 'ruler or cane' . . .

When a question was asked
One put up a hand;
And those with wrong answer
At the front they would stand . . .

Those that misbehaved,
Or found 'all a terrible task',
Would get 'lines' or 'homework',
And 'would be going home last' . . .

From home, a 'baked potato'
Would have been given for lunch -
Not butter nor cheese,
Just a hard-crusted crunch . . .

Or, if you'd spent your lunch-penny,
You'd be seated alone;
And by the end of school day
'How your stomach would groan!' . . .

Happy schooldays -
Don't make me laugh!
Just pick up and study
An 'old' school-group photograph . . .

Mary Pauline Winter (née Coleman)

Bygone Summers

Bygone summers I once knew
A coach setting off in the morning dew.
With our sandwiches and bucket and spade
And at little cost our day was made.
There was Granny and Grandad and Uncle Bill
And Tommy and Rose who lived on the hill.
We were all so excited, it was so hard to contain
Main thing we all hoped we didn't get rain.
We cried with joy when the sea came in sight
Oh yes, this was a perfect day all right.

Anne Churchward

Death Of A Steelworks

Decaying in unfriendly silence,
Wind-torn roof sheets sway,
Broken phone wires swinging madly,
Slowly dying day by day.

Wormwood smothered railway track,
Moss grown, stagnant water tower,
Time clocks where time itself stands still,
Wall grown weeds attempt to flower.

Soot-grimed splintered windowpane,
Rampant grass devouring well-worn paths,
Sagging roofs spill slates at random,
Ageing paintwork split with cracks.

Where are all the sparks and flame
Hot slag that lit the sky at night?
The sweat, the dust, the noise, the heat,
Blinding, scorching, searing light.

Men with sweat cloths hung in belts,
Tools that shone like beaten gold,
Tending, coaxing, molten steel
Rolling, forging, skills of old.

Their knowledge was our future's gain,
Hard thick arms and knowing eye,
Lost now, never to return,
Remember how we let them die.

Stephen John Whitehouse

Memories

I sit here by the window and dream of days gone by
It seems like only yesterday, my how the time does fly
Saturday in winter used to bring me thoughts of joy
I'd go and watch the local lads, that's what one did as a boy.

Before too long when time had passed they'd pick me for the team,
I scored two goals on my debut and thought it was a dream
The winter was soon over, the football season's passed
My father says, 'I'm glad it's done, cricket's here at last.'

I must admit I did agree, my father loved his sport
He never missed a match all year, I know he was that sort
Saturdays were special for Dad, the kids and me
I'm not so sure about our wives, they had to make the tea.

Some days the cricket was over just because of rain
We'd just get back onto the field and down it came again
The season passed quickly, a memorable one at that,
We won the league, a record too, that no one will surpass.

I'm still here by the window with my memories of the past
It's all too soon passed on by and was far too good to last
If time that's passed in all these years was etched out of my brain
I wouldn't worry one little bit, for I'd do it all again.

Roy Smith

Fond Memories Of A Misspent Youth

Sometimes, when in a mellow mood
I think of scenes and times of yore.
Memories are restored in a returning flood
Like dreams from an immortal store.
Carnival was great in that cold northern town
With marching bands in multicoloured hue.
I dreamed of love and settling down
With a pretty girl who played a mean kazoo.
On market nights my spirit slowly warmed
Under old-fashioned flickering oil lamp's flame.
Sarsaparilla and penny dips, my taste buds charmed
Peas pudding, sumptuous saveloys, my youthful appetite to tame.
A glorious, sandy, golden beach was there
Though not much used by all the local folk.
Rides on a chairplane from a nearby fair
And fortune-tellers the fire of youthful dreams to stoke.
A grim, old-fashioned, grey town hall
A throwback to Victorian splendour.
In front, artistic female statues to enthral
Placed there a touch of class to render.
On Friday nights they were to drunken revellers
Free female forms to fondle in the dark.
Until those statues, at the command of unctuous levellers
Were shifted to a distant seaside park.
What wondrous times I spent in my enquiring youth
When I recall my burgeoning immature actions.
But, if you really want to know the awful truth
I much prefer our modern-day attractions!

Jack Scrafton

Nostalgia

In Memory Lane one should take care to make a presentation fair
Old codgers' tales of days gone by are often made with half-shut eye
Life's always eased for wealthy folk, but the deprived still face the yoke
Not long ago each coin was treasure: nowadays most have cash
                                                   for pleasure
Goods once built to last, discarded all too soon,
Today's variety once like crying for the moon.

But some old ways are surely; they've stood the test of time
Showing modern wastage to be something of a crime
Education, for all its cost many essentials have been lost
Too many teachers at wits end, almost driven round the bend
Time was when crime was in control, despite so many on the dole;
Our prisons sought to bring reform; now reoffending is the norm
Murder, once rare, cause for despair; oft undertaken lightly
Nowadays it often seems to claim a victim nightly.

In my young days most citizens prized honesty and honour
Now anything in reach of thief is probably a goner
Some suffered burglars 'tis true, the miscreants unarmed
Some rich men's houses plundered, but the occupants unharmed.

Despite material gains today and spread of real wealth
I doubt if folk are happier, or in better mental health
Wars and threats of violence still make city dwellers fear
Now effects of global warming: menacing all we hold most dear
We need to return to common sense; much less commercial greed
Adopting rules that offer hope, allowing more to feed
One might go on for evermore, but deeds, not words are needed
Quite likely doom will be our lot, without some warnings heeded.

Don Bishop

The Black Horse, Grimsthorpe

Warming by living fire flame
Sitting cosy and content
We reminisce of Christmases gone
And all the joy those times have meant.

Sipped ruby wine from pretty stemmed glass
Admired the decorated tree
Ate our lunch of fine cuisine
It was the perfect place to be.

Through windowpane our eyes beheld
Winter sky - wind-tossed, fallen leaves
And I thanked God for His special gift
The love dear mother, you've given to me.

Sheila Parker

Beyond Debate

The traumas, child and teenage years
Inflicted now are silent dust
In attic mind declines to sort.
And drugs had no appeal. I trust
My wife and feel a sense of pride,
Or thanks at least, at way our boy
And daughters thrive; despite the fact
The former now cannot enjoy
His favoured line, since fall has chained
Him down to trap of chair on wheels.
The minor setbacks in my life
Are soon forgot. My work appeals
And satisfies. In short, I'm free
From angst (if not complacent mien!)
But with-it critic claims I'm left
With nowt to say as poet keen
To capture thoughts and feelings just
To please, inspire or entertain.
For him the night is art's abode.
He praises works I find inane.
He seems to preach a life devoid
Of aim. But I perceive we're called
To be apprentice saints, if slow
To learn that love will get us thralled.
But by its bonds we'll reach a state
Of joy, beyond all paint and hate.
A timeless realm beyond debate.

Henry Disney

Grandma's Old Mug (George V Coronation)

I found Grandma's old mug in the cupboard today
For so many years it lay hidden away
Now it's nearly a hundred years old, I would say
Although there's a maze of cracks in the glaze
The memories it conjures, time cannot erase.

Passed down from my grandmother on to my mother
Who passed it to me - but I didn't bother
About that old mug - it meant nothing to me
I was into 'Blue Ring' and then 'Indian Tree' -
Both of them now as outdated as me!
Whereas Grandma's old mug will soon be an 'antique'
But whatever its value, to me it's unique.

I wonder who drank from it last - was it me
When I was a child at my grandmother's knee?
I remember in those days, the grown-ups drank tea
Or Camp coffee essence with chicory -
It was Ovaltine, cocoa or Oxo for me.

Now I've started to ponder, it's all coming back
When Dad's breakfast was bacon, I had 'bread and fat'
And thought myself lucky to get even that
I ran errands for pennies to spend at the shop
On sherbet dabs, liquorice or lollipops.

After school, for an ice cream us kids would all go
To Bedford's Ice Cream King - Antonio
Then came the war - sweets and fruit disappeared
And I craved a banana all through the war years
When ice cream came back, I wept joyful tears!

Sweets stayed on the ration until forty-nine
And I'd go hunting Mars bars from time to time
I still have a penchant for Mars bars today
Though the recipe's altered, so I've heard say.

Now I've had a few smiles and shed a few tears
Finding Grandma's old mug, after all these years
It will take pride of place in the cupboard for me
And though Grandmother left us in forty-three
It will always hold such precious memories for me.

It won't contain cocoa or Oxo today
But a nice drop of bubbly I've hoarded away
So here's to dear Grandma -
                    Hip hip hip hooray!

Sheila Allen

May Alexander

If you want to come and play
Just go up to Mrs A
She will tell you when to come
To the playscheme that she runs.

Swimming, day trips we would go
Saltcoats, Ayr and Irvine
People we met along the way
Knew we kids all liked to play.

Late at night our venture done
To the station we would run
Chips and rolls and Coke for all
We have surely had a ball.

Thirty years have come and gone
But the playscheme still goes on
Mrs A has retired now
But still remembers all her crowd.

Ann Buchanan

English Dreams

Shared English dreams of halcyon times
Dawn-rattled churns and bell-pulled chimes;
Slabbed cheese and mead in manor fields
Burnt peasant faces, orchard yields.

New labour worked on cotton gins
And smugglers met in Cornish inns;
So Wordsworth gazed on Rydal's Mount
Industrial rich became the count.

Shire horses from a Norfolk scene
The clicks of willow on the green;
The shilling hire, lead-blackened grate
A dusk-tryst by a farmhouse gate.

Range cottage bread, the poorhouse gruel
Rote chanting from the village school;
Clogs myriad trod the cobbled stones
Cut lavender was breath and forest cones.

Embroidered stitch, pared mantle lamps
Brass Sunday bands, red penny stamps;
Then, copperplate was nurtured gift
While saving was encouraged thrift.

Time-trembled skaters on the Thames
Fine ladies drawn in fur-edged hems
Half-hunter watches, dark clasped capes,
Scots Flier and carriages of varied shapes.

Wood powder strewed the butcher's floor
And youth's flower died in total war;
Raised hats acknowledged funeral cars
Still science dreamt of reaching Mars!

Christopher Rothery

Memories

I wake each morning thinking of your smile
The joy, love and devotion you gave me each day
I cherish the memories of those loathsome miles
That we used to sing our songs as we went our way.

I often think of the things we did together
Even if it was nothing but holding hands
Then I can't help but smile to myself
Because of those memories of our future plans.

My love for you seems to grow more each day
As I look at the pictures I have of you
I've grown to love you in every way
I often catch myself crying because I miss you too.

The love and joy you brought into my life
The memories I use to get me through each night and day
I know we often talked about you being my wife
Now that you're gone your memories start me on my way again today.

William Lacewell Jnr

Sharing

Sharing was part of our lives
Friday night sweets for after chip suppers
Saturday lunch, pies or sometimes fritters
Yorkshires on Sunday and slices of beef
Mmm, home-baked puddings and cakes.

Warm hot cross buns, Easter eggs all round
Toffee filled for Dad, milk chocs for Mum
We'd open ours carefully for buttons or sweets
Simnel cake, fluffy chicks, chocolate nests
Easter biscuits and yummy treats.

Christmas store cupboard and making the cake
Planning recipes and mince pies to bake
Shopping and wrapping, put up the tree
Sharing all these pleasures the family and me
All sharing the past good things in life.

Julia Fitzpatrick

Gone Are The Days

Thursday night is here once more
With hunger knocking at the door
So out we go to do our shop
We push the trolleys till we drop

Gone are the days when we'd be served
Our favourite ham that'd just been cured
And stand with sawdust by our feet
And watch the butcher cut his meat.

Now we rush from shelf to shelf
Choosing in haste, without any help
Filling our trolleys with hardly a thought
Amazed at the end at what we have bought.

Gone are the days when we'd have the say
At just what amount we wanted that day
We'd have time to talk to friends as we shopped
As gossip and news was eagerly swapped.

But either way, it has to be done
Even the queue cannot be shunned
And when we get through we drive home in the car
Cos gone are the days when our shops weren't so far.

Christine Shelley

Old Friends

Life is just a fleeting glance
That passes all too quick
We either know great happiness
Or just a little chink.

Growing old has been no fun
Our laughter turned to tears
We moan as we watch the sun
Set on our passing years.

But friendship is a thing we know
For just a little while
May we meet again some day
When we have learned to smile.

Elizabeth Murray Shipley

A Special Lady, Ivy

As we say goodbye to you today
We all have so much more to say
You loved your grandchildren visiting
And spoilt them when staying.

You knitted all the school jumpers
And often made a rice pudding for afters
You walked across the park to Took's shop
Generously giving most away before you stop.

You crazed for scratchcards and were very lucky
Uncovering your prize using your fingernails happily
You loved Felixstowe and the amusement arcade
And were always proud of how much you had made.

You would use the telephone every night
Sharing all the latest gossip with delight
You would knock your leg without knowing this
And visited a day-centre, never to miss.

You wrote the birthday cards months ahead
And always missed what was said
We all have fond memories of a special lady
Always pleased with the arrival of a baby.

We know you didn't like being alone
And loved to hear a vocal tone
We are proud of your achievements
As we remember all of your life's events.

Adrian Bullard

Night Train To Berlin - Alexanderplatz

Night train to Berlin - Alexanderplatz
Unknown stations flicker by,
I see your reflection, blessing my fortune
Then shivering for I realise
Everything beautiful comes to an end
And from high up on the ugly, yet majestic Fernsehturm,
We view a myriad neon lights
From the sprawling metropolis below.

I reflect on the horror here before
In the dark days of the Second World War

And all the petty dramas enacted now
The same themes in any language.
We cross the Spree and enter a bar
Drinking Pilsner into the early hours.
Night train to Berlin - Alexanderplatz
A name to grace any poem,
These magical hours swiftly glide
Yet I feel a tinge of sadness for

Everything beautiful comes to an end
I dread a broken heart which cannot mend.

Guy Fletcher

A Harston Childhood - 1923+

I'm in my second childhood, that's what it's called by men
And now I can have all the things I couldn't afford back then.
Back in my very early years there were no computer games,
No TV or videos, but we managed just the same.

We rode our fairy cycles, we had our rollerskates,
Whips and tops and skipping in the street with all our mates.
Marbles in the playground, handstands against a wall
Hanging from a tree branch; perhaps that's what made me tall!

Swimming in the river (the Cam was clean back then),
No crime or interference from 'less than perfect' men,
House doors were always open, there was no petty theft,
'Look, on the kitchen table, see the gift someone has left!'

Vegetables from their garden, 'What to give in return?'
'I know, we've got a pile of logs, far more than we can burn.'
Little things in today's world, but it's the way we used to be
In a village not far from Cambridge, that means childhood to me!

J M Jones

Memory

What a precious gift our memory is
Especially when we're older
Sitting alone on a winter's night
The weather getting colder
In a cosy room on a comfy chair
We can turn it on at will
All at once the past is there
And the room begins to fill
With all the enjoyments we have had
Together with our mum and dad
Friends and relatives are with us too
Remembering things we used to do
The best of happenings we have shared
Some of them happy, some of them sad
Oh, what a pleasure to relive
All the things we said and did
What a precious gift our memory is.

Jean Salmon

School Reunion

Behold! The prating ladies,
The well-remembered faces,
Disguising with clever hand
The lines and wrinkled traces.
Greying tresses haute-coiffured;
Styles defying gravity!
Quizzical eyes raised . . . rouged lips
Twitching pert with levity.

View the chattering monkeys,
Seeking to capture lost youth,
Whilst a few keep to themselves
In corners, nervous, aloof.
The sparkling eyes . . . memories
Extracted from distant past.
The scenario is set,
The leading players are cast!

Behold! The prating ladies,
The extra pound's weight noted!
Sizing up and eyeing up,
Their make-up thickly coated.
The flushed and shiny faces
Turning this and ev'ry way,
To catch the ear of a friend,
Determined to have their say!

Voices raised high in laughter,
Back and forth in waves of sound,
All vying for centre-stage,
Old photos passing around.
Sweet be the remembrance!
Sisterly pacts and friendship,
In school assembly standing,
Their voices raised in worship.

See the trailing crocodile
Marching on the battlefield,
Eyeing their adversaries,
Hockey sticks in hand they wield.
The clash of the bully-off!
Echoing down twenty years,
Heading for the goals of life,
Mayhap, success laced with tears.

Girlish camaraderie
Keen to relate their story,
Let them happily recall
Their brief moment of glory
Before venturing homeward,
Nursing old dreams and wishes
Which, sadly, tend to end with
A sink of dirty dishes!

Gwendoline Douglas

Past Times

In the still of the night
You came holding the candle
With its flame
Throwing shadows in the
Corners of my mind
Revealing all the memories
Once again that were lost in
The ever running sands of time
In the still of the night
I see you
The candle and its light?
In the shadows of my mind
You lighten all the back
Roads as I walk
Into past times.

V N King

Shaping Our Lives

Have you ever really thought
That by others we are taught?
Things we do gleaned from past friends
Traditions from those whose passing never ends
That special bond carried on through our lives
Ensures the warmth of shared friendship survives
We dwell on thoughts of this and that
Hints we valued from a friendly chat
Each time appreciated memories we repeat
Those quirks which make our lives complete
With lingering thoughts we retain those times
Adapting our ways to those our memory mimes.

Betty Bukall

The Big Fish

Children down at the coast for a treat
A fisherman mending his net they did meet
He started telling them a very long tale
Of the fish he caught as big as a whale
At sea he set up his fishing rod and got a bite
To haul it in he tried with all his might
He tied the line to his boat to take a short rest
To escape the big fish was doing its best
The fish was so strong, it was towing the boat
Knowing to land it he had little hope
The line was too tight to be unwound
There was no help and no one around
His boat was being dragged down by this fish
To get out of trouble was the fisherman's wish
'God no more will I fish if I get home safe.'
At that very moment the line did break
I was then able to get back safely to the shore
I now sit and mend nets and fish no more.

L A G Butler

The Absent Friend

I always thought we'd be friends forever
Come rain, come shine, come stormy weather
Whatever I did, you had my back
In retrospect, it don't mean jack
Because in a puff of smoke, it all went sour
Where was my friend in my darkest hour?
Out of the blue, you just cut me dead
What did I do? Did I mess with your head?
There was no discussion and there was no row
At the time it hurt me, you spiteful cow
I tried to make contact, you never answered my calls
I was left wondering, was I a fool?
Holidays stopped, so did nights out in clubs
Dinner parties we had and drinks down the pub.
Although I've moved on and friends I have new
Sometimes, occasionally I think of you
And if you ever read this, then I wish you well
And I thank you for giving me this story to tell.

Lisa Knight

My Linda

The other day I remembered
How I used to love my Linda
She was so special
In every sort of way
She would come to me
In my dreams
And hold me close
I never imagined she would go away
We were a couple
That dreamed our days away
And she always used to tell me
All the things I wanted to hear
I remembered her blue eyes
Gleaming when she looked me in the eye
And the day she said goodbye
Part of me vanished with her.

Muhammad Khurram Salim

Beaches

When you think of beaches
They are usually in far-out reaches.
Warm, white and sandy between the toes
Coarse, rocky and stony, a 'frown' begins to show.

No children on them about to engage in play
The beaches I refer to, were not so far away.
Ridden with dead and dying, upon the shores of France
The blood they shed was *poppy-red,* they never had a chance.

The graves of fallen soldiers, the memory still with us yet
The time of former glory, 'lest we forget'.
There are white crosses in the sand where the brave men fell
They will not be forgotten if our children we tell.

There is laughter now on beaches everywhere
Children act out their dreams
They dig with spades, build castles with buckets
The Channel is their stream.
There is bashing and smashing, giggling and fun
Where once upon a time, men with bravery fought and won.

Ellen Spiring

Pictures Speak A Thousand Words

The magic of photography fascinates me,
Freedom to look at any subject in all sincerity;
When you look through the viewfinder, what do you see?
An image to be preserved for posterity.

A thousand words each picture can speak,
Moments captured in time for you to keep;
Even when your memories begin to grow weak,
Sweet thoughts into your brain will start to seep.

There's your beloved first pet and you as a child,
A glorious afternoon, so long ago,
Beside you stands your mother, so gentle and kind,
But where the years have gone, you don't know.

Snapshots of visits to so many places
Evoke feelings of mischievousness and fun;
Dancing eyes and sunburnt faces
Signalling that summer holidays had begun.

A baby's smile or a lover's tender gaze,
Sublime images which will never age;
But you long to go back and revisit those days
Instead of just slowly turning each page.

Annabelle Tipper

Thirteen Tattered Floors Above

'what a child may say can change your life'
she said as we sat on the tattered terrace
of a dank building I never loved
and went to each Thursday because I loved her
amid the distant hum of traffic
that stood seething thirteen tattered floors below
and the innocence of little sparrows
that came visiting bits of my cold sandwich
she and I spoke words that I now know shall last
because I did meet such a child
what a child may say can change your life
it did mine

Vee Sharma

In Loving Memory Of My Dear Big Brother, Father And Friend, Norman

Oh Norman, what a big brother, father and friend
You have been to me, also in the past,
You have always given good advice that will last and last.
And of all the illnesses you have fought so hard to overcome
And in the end you peacefully did succumb.
When Alice died how I cried and cried of my strife
Oh how you helped to get on with my life.
And now that you have died, how I have cried and cried
Until my tears have dried
Again of our friendship of the past
You have always been so good and true.
And never again will be able to renew.
Of your two sons they have always been so good to me
And always thought I was on your family tree
Oh Norman, how I will miss you as a big brother, father and friend
Your loss will take time to mend.
Of your friendship I have been so glad
I know at times I have made you a little mad
This exciting life of the past you have always led
And now that you have shed.
Now I have one thought in mind,
And how to other people you have been so very kind.
Of the Mann family, how you have helped them through their strife
Although you knew the ebbing of your life was so near,
And with it you held your life so dear.
You helped their children of your commuter skills,
How well you taught them and it gave you such admiration and thrills
Here again I say, how you have helped so many people in the past.
I am sure they will always think of you in their thoughts
That will last and last.
How I counted our blessings of the past
Of knowing you and as I look into the sky and think of the past
And to my mind it will forever last.
And that your life has come to cease
May your soul rest in everlasting peace.

Peter Antonian

All Things Considered

Life's not been bad;
all things considered.

Felt sad when our Jim died
- cried and cried.
But that were the war.

I were a lass when we wed
and then 'e were dead.

But it could've been worse.

Four little mouths
I worked all hours
No time to think

Just as well really.

Here I am now . . .
nice little flat
easy to keep
but heating's
not cheap
and the lift
dun always work.

But life's not been bad;
all things considered.

Sylvia Fairclough

I Wonder If The Meadow Still Exists . . .

I wonder if the meadow still exists where, as a child,
I wandered, by a brook ankle-deep in damp grass I played
Picking clover, sucking honey from its stems.

Does the warm-remembered meadow still remain
Or have they turned the turf a small estate to build
Where children live?

It has happened in so many lovely places
With no safe haven left for play and dreams
No birdsong there to entertain them
With trees and hedges gone to scaffolding.

We may have given them a place to live
But simple beauty sacrificed her soul
And now they sit indoors and watch a screen of violence and stupidity.

We have robbed them of their dreams
And childhood dreams are precious ones indeed
And may be given reign, their thoughts to roam
While dabbling bare toes in silver streams.

So do not drown this green and pleasant land in concrete
Stone and brick and harsh cement
But leave some meadow places, sweet, unspoiled
So children may play and dream to heart's content.

If our lives are not enriched by natural things
How can our children learn to love and respect?
The poorer then our nation will become
When only harsh imaginings go unchecked.

Ida Jones

My Coal Fire

My coal fire that I miss, it was simply bliss
To toast your bread by the fire
Spread with lovely beef dripping, Jack Frost your toes nipping
Enjoyed with hot scalding tea
You banked up the fire to keep cosy and warm
Against the cold which could do your harm
Sometimes for us, it was crumpets instead
Whatever it was, thankfully we were well fed
For seventeen shillings, a ton of best coal
To the cellar which was tipped down a hole
With the coming of boilers you had to buy anthracite
(Which was really coke)
Your bath at night the only was for hot water on tap
Then to sit by the fire with a cat on your lap
Toasting your legs until the fire got too fierce
In later years could cost you dear
Yet to see the fire as you came in the door
Lifted your spirits even if you were poor
For it meant that there was food on your table to make a meal of sorts
A gas fire is not the same, ah but what is in a name?
Yet remembering the cosy fireside chair
The people around you, oh so dear
The dance band on the old-fashioned wireless
Up to the wooden hill, down sheet lane
Covered by blankets and a counterpane.
While the wind whistled and down came the rain
A cup of hot milk and a cosy bed and a lovely soft pillow
To lay our head on . . . oh memories!

Rosemary Peach

Upon Her Clarion Call

Dropping from trees
scrambling through hedges
flying across tarmac
jets racing to cover

Screaming along runways
spread-eagling dawdlers
refuelling, peering out
over creaking drawbridges

Filtering sounds
scanning horizons
being still
anxiously waiting for Miss

Martin Conway

I Love You, Miss You And Will Never Forget You

I have sat here before, watching the world go by,
With every breath I gave a big sigh,
And tried my hardest not to cry,
Wondering why you had to die.

Slowly time has eased the pain,
Sometimes it still hurts to say your name,
Although life can never be the same,
I am beginning to live again.

Julie Marie Laura Shearing

Eating Ice Cream On A Winter's Day

Chattering of teeth
Icy waft against the face
Arctic breath billows smoke signals
Biting vanilla pods freeze the tongue
Glacial cheeks red raw
Frosty gums white from the coolness inside
Bitter fingers hold crisp cone
Polar air breathes in and out.

H H Martinez

Old Hill Town

Old Hill Town is changing
Factories around closing
New houses they are building
Landmarks once scarred
Flattened and cleared

A changing town
Many times round
More greenery to be found
Is for the better
Or even matter?

For me too old you see
What will be will be
Others to have a say
In the future maybe one day

Old Hill Town will still be there
This we can all declare!

Garry Bedford

Recollections

In recollections of my past
I look back to my childhood days,
Days of sublime happiness
Culminating in fun-filled times
Any untoward mistakes forgotten
Any wrong-doing erased from memory
Then was a time of family togetherness
Brothers and sisters, each other's benefactors
Alas, brothers and sisters now gone
A void hard to redeem.

To mourn them would be natural
But to mourn them unfortunate
I look back with a smile
They may be gone
But they have left me a legacy
A legacy of good fortune
The satisfaction and gratification
That we lived, laughed and strove together
Nothing can ever take those memories away
They remain vivid pictures in my thoughts.

In retrospect I recall these good times
To dwell on any unhappy incidents
I believe to be a blight on their memory
Happiness uplifts the spirit
And I rejoice in the knowledge
(Even though they are here no more)
They still live in my heart and soul
Giving me a feeling of rich contentment
And the gratification
Of a past worth reawakening.

To live in the past
Must never be confused
With thinking of the past
Life has to go on
Of that there is no doubt
To think of the past
Can often bring to prominence
An outstanding incident
Which in its own way
Brought joy or relief
Which resurfaces in the active mind.

Family values in this day and age
Are very often scoffed at
But in my active reminiscences
The pictures convey joy
Comradeship and old-fashioned ties
If any of the family fell out of step
The rest would rally to his/her aid
Harmonising into focus
The need for conciliation
And togetherness
Most of all - *love.*

W G Stannard

Women - Big Changes

Walking down my memory lane
When sweet love changed everyone's life again,
Chilling memories of a historical past
Bringing big changes to women especially, at last!

On the 6pm News Churchill said it was war,
Our lives as we knew them were no more,
All men and women for action would go,
Join all the forces to fight the foe.

Jobs, men left, many women would train,
Family life would never be the same again.
To the country for safety went children from the city,
With rationing and coupons for everything, what a pity!

In the tough 'Land Army' our food women grew,
Farmers said, 'Without them what would we all do?'
Well together we all worked and together we won,
May today's women front liners,
Show this world what should be done!

Stella Bush-Payne

Night Errant

Summer nights have evocativeness for me
Recently I was thinking of you in the garden at dusk
When the trees and hedges perfumed the night greenly.

At two or three in the morning we ambled separately
And side by side through the lanes to my house
The light was silvery grey and the shadows deep
A world turned into black and white film
Monochrome dramatised and simplified.

Our relationship was childlike and giggly
The implications of our moonlit stroll did not intrude
Into the bubble where we walked and kissed.

It was warm and moths flickered in the soft air
As we talked of books and films and drinks
There was a freedom in it, a lack of consequence
Which was always the gift you gave people
There was a confidence in it
Which seems unjustified now
Since I know we did not have a rosy future.

Without hurrying we would arrive at my door and whisper goodnight
And I would step through the door to a world of colour.

Chris Madelin

Blackberries In Autumn

(For Max - the Staffordshire bull terrier)

I won't be picking blackberries this year
Now that you're not here
They ripened prematurely, just like you left
Too soon
And I should treat this maturely
Because you would not want me to be sad
Only for me to be glad
Of all the days we shared
And how much we loved and cared
Remember how we made wine
My brother and I with you watching nearby?
You ate blackberries, they went down a sweet treat
And the autumn sun shone over you
I tried to hide the tears I wept as you left
I kissed you goodbye with a gentle sigh
And the sun that fell over you
Was the sunlight straight from Heaven.

C A Keohane-Johnson

Snapshots Of The Past

It feels strange looking back at photos
Of Mum and Dad so young.
Dad in his army khaki,
A forties ballad being sung?

Then there's Grandma and Grandad
Taken in the First World War.
Mum a small child at their feet,
I wonder what Grandad saw?

Great-Grandma looks severe and prim
Wearing black and hair pulled taut.
Her face shows not a hint of a smile,
What sort of hardship had she fought?

Then my wedding day, to baby smiles
And cheeky boyish grins to men.
My precious album is almost complete
Except for grandchildren - when?

Margaret Rowe

Of Teatime Teas

O Sunday and Sunday teas
Pickles, ham, tomatoes, Spam,
Pure wholemeal bread
And teatime tea and cheese
Worries cease, a cream bun feast
Fruit and veg aplenty
Loaf and butter, here I stutter
Times like these cease to be
Yet there's a girl who given a whirl
Reminds me so easily
That pickle, ham, tomatoes and jam
Are our England's cup of victory.

R J Collins

Memories

As we go through life we just live day by day
Taking the good times with the bad
Sometimes we have much happiness
Other times we will be sad
Most people get a mixture
But just occasionally
The equation is off balance
And we get a lot of misery.
However, when we reminisce
As we get older we tend to do
We like to dwell on the good times
That's what I do . . . do you?
It's like the empty glass syndrome
Is it half empty or half full?
If you try to stay positive
I follow this simple rule
My wee sister died of cancer
Despite five years of fear and operations
Even towards the end . . . in the hospice . . .
We used to find humour in situations
When we chatted about the old days
Though at the time they weren't funny
As our childhood had been wartime
All the rationing and little money
So often it was the wee silly things
That gave us such a laugh
So we used to cheer up the old folk
And she was popular with the staff.

Mary Scott

No Place Like Home

A tin of delights filled with sweets
Sunday afternoon sideboard treats
Home-made lemonade not alone
Ginger beer stands in jars of stone.

Home-made cakes, bread pudding for tea
Jam on the stove, bubbling so free
The whistle of the kettle, a table to lay
The joyful sounds of children in play.

Dandelion and burdock, toffee apple licks
Bags of sugar with rhubarb sticks
Bygone treats from a bygone age
Disappear as the book of life turns the page.

Jacket potatoes, toast on the fire
The heart of the house, flames get higher
Fireside stories with rose-coloured glasses?
Different tales from different classes.

Life flows on, enjoy it while you can
Simple pleasures of home, no master plan
For wherever you may go, wherever you may be
There is no place like home, believe me.

Geoffrey Meacham

Teenage Afternoons Remembered

A Sunday roast
And the prison of overeaten apathy
A pre-war matinee
Seen in a haze
From the back-achingly comfortable sofa.

A time for the hobbies I never had
When frustration let loose
Behind a gingerly locked bedroom door
In a torrent of self-abuse
Left me exhausted upon the shore
Of this becalmed afternoon sea
When time is forever
A quarter to three.

And I would wait through
This suburban malaise
Until the new week flicked its eyelids open
With 'Songs of Praise'.

Matthew Hustings

A Journey

People - many people 'drop off' the carousel of life
Old friends - treasured friends, special people
Leaving not much but memories
Of happy times - sad times - testing times
These people were a part of us, our lives
Smile on the moment
Greet it with all your senses
Let not the passing of time rob you
Of the brief pleasure it brings
Carefree like a butterfly on a summer's day
And then . . . all too soon . . . away
Such moments of pleasure never to return
Here to see autumn's touch of gold
To know mornings bright, crisp and fresh
The white sheet of winter long and cold
And spring with spirits, new and bright
Things change but the memory remains
As we travel down memory lane
With absent friends, things and times gone.

Clive Cornwall

Precious Memories

In the good old days our family was complete
However, our son David's sudden passing
Knocked the world from beneath our feet.

A parent's worse nightmare had somehow come true
One never expects a child to pass before you.

Such a devastating loss, no words can explain
As we turn our thoughts over in our minds once again.

Such a tragic waste of a life
He was a master craftsman too
However, God had decided to call him to rest
When He chose our son David
He certainly picked the best.

You will never be forgotten
We thought the world of you
David, you are only ever a thought away
Lovingly remembered every step
Along life's way.

Joan Igesund

Foot In The Door

I'm closer to sixty than fifty
Perhaps I live a little in the past
I keep thinking about the yesterdays
The good times I thought would always last
By growing up alongside your friends
You put meaning into the words 'best mates'
Everyone respected and loved each other
If someone was in need, you wouldn't dare be late
The modern world runs at a cut-throat pace
The younger generation is under so much strain
With the cost of living, caught in the fast lane
The kids of today experience society's pain
I'm closer to sixty than fifty
I remember when there were job opportunities galore
I worked hard withstanding life's pressures
But sadly today, it's hard to get a foot in the door.

Russell Mortimer

These Are The Days Of My Life!

When I was young in every boutique I would go shopping
Each week I would spend all my money without stopping!
Buying tank-tops and miniskirts, that barely covered my thighs
Blouses and shift dresses made of psychedelic dyes!
Sloppy-Joe jumpers from my neck to my knees
Bell-bottom trousers that blew in the breeze.
Winkle pickers, high heels that made me look tall
Platform sole shoes off of which I would fall.
I wanted to look like Twiggy and Mary Quant
With white knee-high boots and my hair in a bouffant!

Then into the 70s came the flower power sense
The fashion went crazy, you know what I mean.
Hippies and Beatniks wanted to make love not war
And wanted to take their bells and beads to Glastonbury Tor.
Some went as far as living in a tent
You could say it was the days that anything went.

So when ABBA came along and set a new fashion trend
With hotpants and catsuits in which you could hardly bend.
Frilly shirts and smart suits all in white
Feather boas and hats that you pulled down tight.

Freddie Mercury also made an impact on the fashion scene
With crazy outfits that he wore when singing with Queen.
So as from his song, 'The Days Of Our Lives'
I'd wear it all again and I would not think twice!

Because way back then in the fashion I always wanted to be
But nowadays all I think about
Are my cosy slippers and a nice cup of tea.
It's not that I don't like today's latest fashion dress
It's now that I'm a nan I no longer need to dress to impress!

Sue Dancey

Round The Table

Around the room a familiar scene
Eyes fast-glued to the plasma screen
Food being eaten automatically
What do they taste? What do they see?
Each cocooned in their own little world
As drama and tragedy on the screen is unfurled
In the dimly lit room it's almost surreal
Can they tell if it's home-cooked or a ready meal?
It may be a takeaway ordered in haste
Indian, Chinese or Thai, whatever their taste
They sit and they sit as if they are glued
Surrounded by the debris of paper plates and fast food
How I long to return to those days long ago
When we sat at a table with everything just so
Conversation was interesting, no TV to intrude
As we saw what we ate, enjoying our food
Our parents told us their stories of days long past
We sat there entranced and wished time could last
Remembering good old days as their history they told
Life's treasured memories, more precious than gold
Those bygone days vanished forever I'm sure
Suddenly I hear a knock on the door
It's the delivery man with a takeaway meal
So, I join in with the young ones, I have to get real
The TV switched on, I sit with my tray
A familiar scenario, like a fast-forward replay
Customs are changing, sadly I feel,
Even the food, it doesn't taste real
Communication is lacking in so many ways
How I long for those meals round the table in the good old days.

Brenda Hughes

A Memory To Share

It's 1967 and the world has gone mad
That's in the opinion of my so-square dad
Flower power had arrived but not so as you would know
For nothing in our house would tell you so
My dad had opinions on everything
Not in his day would you see such goings on
He blamed the government
They should put all the youths in the army
And bring back conscription
Plenty of jobs were to be had, a time when life was great
Money had real value, food was always plentiful
Real meat was on the plate
Saturday nights were special as you went out on the town
Hipsters, flowery shirts and ties
Dad said all you need is a red nose to look just like a clown
Dad was the original Grumpy Old Man
He didn't go with the flow, he didn't understand the master plan
It's 40 years since power came and went
But all in all a good time spent
Dad has now gone to a place in which he didn't believe
I can hear him now grumbling and moaning at everything
Growing up in the 60s, I am glad I was there
Memories are special, we all like to share.

Charles Trail

Looking Back

Seasons always used to be very stratified
'Hot summers, cold winters' . . . is what they sigh
Though some data shows which doesn't lie
It *has* been like this before in years gone by
Lifestyles changing throughout the years
Wearing strangest clothes without a fear
It was the current trends and *was* 'hip gear'
Quite embarrassing now, that's quite clear.
It was normal to have a manual job
And you could get most things for about two bob
Any more and you felt you were being robbed
Abuse the police, you'd get smacked in the gob
Now it's Superstores - not corner shops
A million pounds for football flops
Genetic foods from cultured crops
The pace increases and never stops
Let's embrace and go with these new trends
Enjoy our different cultured friends
See the Internet as being a very good spend
As if we 'go back' the world might end!

Chris Leith

Childhood Memories Of The 1950s

Picking bluebells in the woods, on bright spring days in May.
Knocking on my friend's front door, 'Are you coming out to play?'
We cycled on such quiet roads, not much traffic to be seen,
We had our first TV set then to view the coronation of the Queen.
Sweets were just off ration then our teeth still white and strong.
School holidays passed too quickly and winters seemed so long.
We built enormous snowmen too, they seemed to last for weeks.
And in that snowbound weather, we all had rosy cheeks.
We made our own amusements and staged adventures through
the day.
In summer, in the farmer's barn, we'd play amongst the hay.
Tag, hopscotch and whip the top; simple pleasure we all had.
Blowing bubbles, paper windmills, I can't remember being sad.
We always had fresh fruit and veg, straight from my father's plot.
I loved the melons and the strawberries, quite often scoffed the lot!
Gooseberry tarts and crumbles, were my all-time favourites too
And Mother's apple dumplings; preceded by a tasty stew.
Beef was full of flavour then, cows grazed on luscious grass
And chickens had their feathers on, I learned to pluck them - fast.
But there is one thing that hasn't changed, before we reached
our teens,
My children and myself, you know, all hated eating greens!

Ann Potkins

Sweet Romance

S weet romance where are you?
W here are you sweet romance?
E yes search to find your beauty
E ach day I long to glance
T hose sweet innocent courtships.

R oses held as maiden sighs
O n handsome beau's arm strolling
M aking way with star-filled eyes
A s heart strings play love's rhapsody
N eath moonlight's silv'ry beam
C ome back once more sweet romance
E ros longs to greet his queen.

Violet Corlett

Once Upon A Time

I once was known as a tomboy,
Climbing and running in the woods my style.
Minutes and hours meant nothing to me,
I just stayed in the woods for a while.
Wasn't much bothered by mud splatters,
For I was never out to impress.
Wasn't interested in fashion,
Just cross that I wore a dress.
That really was my fun time,
I wish it hadn't gone away.
When did I stop running in the woodlands?
When did this child cease to play?
Suddenly I was tormented,
Spots had appeared on my face.
Walked lonely in my teenage years
And always felt a disgrace.
I forgot all the fun in the woodlands,
Forgot the wind tossing my hair.
Many years dragged by so slowly,
As I sank in a mire of despair.
My memories have bypassed the sad times,
I can go back to the times that were fun.
To where I played in the woods on my ownsome,
Kicked the leaves and in freedom could run.
God has taught me to accept imperfections,
My hair again is oft out of place,
In my prayers I can hear my lost laughter
That for years had been sadly misplaced.
My spirit now does the running,
I close my eyes and in spirit I know
My spirit is free now and forever
And in spirit I can let myself go.

Rosie Hues

A Fair Affair

When I was a boy it was a joy
To visit the old funfairs
Beneath the stars in dodgem cars
You could drive away your cares.

Roundabout bells and carousels
And the caterpillar ride
Where many a Miss would bestow a kiss
As she snuggled by your side.

Another chance to find romance
Was on the old ghost train
A kiss on the cheek, a feminine shriek
And a slap which brought you pain.

The coconut shy with prizes piled high
Fruit machines by the score
A bag full of chips that burnt your lips
As you wandered home once more.

Good times could be had when I was a lad
At the funfair on the moor
I hadn't much cash on trinkets to splash
But still I was happy, if poor.

Terence Iceton

Singapore

A little copper coin with rounded corners:
I found it lying on the floor one day.
I picked it up
And I remembered

A little island, nestling in the ocean,
As small as seemed the coin upon the floor,
So far away
A love remembered.

Graham Saxby

My Great Love

Nineteen sixty-four was a great year for me
I bought my first Irish Setter called Kerry
Two weeks later I bought another, her name was Gem
Little did I know what I had in store with them.

Nineteen sixty-four and years that followed, what fun
My favourite dogs became well known by everyone
We went to shows, won prizes galore
Also did obedience and won prizes for evermore.

We bred a few litters and kept one more
My son chose one and trained in the park
Sometimes we were up with the lark
Their red coats shining in the sun.

The dogs on the park at play
We walked through woods, the sun gleaming with rays
Such beauty, be it summer or winter shimmering in the sun
Birds singing, squirrels climbing up trees.

Beauty is everywhere when your dog is by your side
We visited hospitals and old people's homes with pride
And when the time came to say goodbye
Because of illness or old age, we must give them a try.

What they gave us, affection, love and a peaceful end
And remember memories live on forever in our hearts
The sixties were certainly very happy years
As I walked down memory lane, writing this with a few tears.

Joan Read

Memories

Many times I've wandered down memory lane
Looking back on happy days when we were young again
Many times I think of all my dearest friends that I once knew
Walking down the memory lane can be fun or sad
So many faces have now gone
Time waits for no man, just the moon shines like it used to
So many things stay the same, raindrops
The spring and summer still arrive on time
Memories are precious, private thoughts of bygone days
Of our loved ones that have gone
Yes, many times I've walked down that lane
Thinking of the days when my golden hair has gone
It's silver now, memories of long ago keep them new
For memories never grow old, only we grow old
Remembering keeps you young and our loved ones close.

Georgette Poole

A Tribute To A Dear Friend

I can't believe you're *seventy!*
It doesn't seem right at all
Your elegance never surprises me
To me, you're the belle of the ball.
We've been good friends since the seventies
Where we taught at Ryeish Green
We had great fun in the staffroom
Repartee - the daily scene.
Then you moved up north to Yorkshire
'Mongst the moors and sweet fresh air
To a year-long labour of love
Where others wouldn't dare
Reconstructing a fine old manor house
Now with Ian taking his share.
No wonder we all love and admire you
For your attitude so rare
Let's drink a toast to our dear friends
To a life full of joy and of care
For we can't drink to one without the other
They have gone where no others would dare.

Valma Streatfield

A Walk Down Memory Lane

It might seem inane but often I enjoy
A walk down memory lane, that first kiss, and
Love letters, a long list with at the end
SWALK as the endearing legend
Soon heading for a lovely wedding in the end.

That first child and a party wild!
Girl or a boy if healthy, can only enjoy . . .
Make a circle of friends engaged in similar ends
At life's ups and downs don't cavil
As along the rough and smooth paths we travel
Holidays we'd take, jolly days, seaside sun bake
Building castles with bucket and spade
Eating our picnic, in some place with shade!

Eventually stretch out, journeying the
Continent about, enjoying foreign fare
Spaghetti Bolognese, lasagne, frogs' legs
And snails challenged Britannia, felt also the glow
Of famous Bordeaux, Logis de France suited our dough
France, Italy, Germany and Spain, we targeted again and again
Sampled knackwurst, on all the sauces quenched our thirst and
Wines from the coolest cellar accompanied our paella.

Overall content, we strengthened our lengthened links
With the continent, raised three cheers
As common marketeers! Drank their health
With various wines and light lager beers
Memories remain which we never disdain, for
We're happy carolling love's old sweet refrain
Joyfully strolling down memory lane.

Graham Watkins

A Walk Down Memory Lane

Memory lane how times have changed
My fondest memories dear
Is my now absent friend
What a welcoming sight in heart and mind
Whenever I needed a friend
She was never hard to find
She was there in times of sadness
She always cared and understood
Whenever I needed a shoulder to cry on
She always did whatever she could.
But now she's gone
Fondest memories always from now on
Be it a love, a partner or a friend
I don't think my heart will ever, ever mend
Times are changing, that's for sure
The good old days are not here anymore
Christmas times are memories always to treasure
Especially the snowflakes a-falling
Oh, what glorious weather!
Robin redbreasts singing with great awe
Carol-singers knocking at our doors
Family you meet on those special festive days
What wonderful parties that we used to have
Happy memories of our wonderful mum and dad
Times have changed
As the years have passed by
I often sit down with sadness
Put my head in my hands and cry
Family have gone, my best friend too
Always forever remembering you!

Mary Woolvin

Stirrings From The Past

Music flowed into the room
Like streams into the river,
Casting rhythms in the heart
Setting souls aquiver.
And with the flow toes tapped the floor
Resounding ancient beat
As music flowed into the room
Making the round complete.
Strings were plucked with golden hands
And strummed with rhythmic force,
And violins were stroked on strings
Like waves upon their course,
And with the flow the Irish drum,
Resounding ancient beat,
Joined in the stream of music notes
Making the round complete.
Three musicians played as one
With stirrings from the past,
Lifting people's hearts and minds
With memories that will last.

Linda Knight

Memory Lane

When we were small, we waved to others
Going to school with sisters and brothers

Some were tall, some were short
Carried bags, full up, left room for thought
We greeted each other with smiles and grins
Talked to friend before class begins.

The teacher gave us work to do
Some work old, some work new
At breaktime with friends we played our games
Was that the bell, oh what a shame
Back into class for lessons new
Finding out there were quite a few.

When day at school had come to end
Mum met us and our friends
Home to tea with time to spare
Out to play with friends who care.

Boys climbed or kicked a ball
Girls skipped, mind you didn't fall
Others on swings or playing a game
Some with conkers, claiming their fame
Making plans for days ahead
Just in time, it was time for bed.

Home we all went sleepy and tired
All our energies had expired
Ready to start another day
Learning and playing, there was no other way.

Jean Smith

Is That Me?

I see a young girl
Who is playing happily
With two younger brothers
Is that me?

I see a girl at school
With her many friends
Too soon she is leaving
As her schooldays end
Is that me?

I see a girl at work
Showing visitors around
The factory where she worked
In the east of the town
Is that me?

I see a young woman in love
With her boyfriend at her side
Soon walking down the aisle
Who was the blushing bride?
Was that me?

I see a mum with children
They numbered three in all
Who enjoyed being a mum
So many tales she can recall
Yes, that was me!

Now I am a grandma
Who has seen heartache and pain
But has many happy memories
And would do it all again
That is me.

Doreen Hampshire

Just A Memory

No one can know
How I miss you so
Life's not the same
Since you had to go.

I'm sure you came
From Heaven above
Cos all your life
You gave me your love.

You were so beautiful
So full of charms
It seemed for ever
You stayed in my arms.

It was so unfair
That we had to part
It was never intended
Not at the start.

But life had a way
Of spoiling our dreams
The strongest of lovers
Must part - so it seems.

Now there's one consolation
That always stays true
It's the beautiful - lasting
Memory of you.

Martin Selwood

The Cornish Farm

After leaving college, I lived on a Cornish farm, deep within a wood
There was no bathroom or running water
Just fields full of cows chewing cud
Miles from anywhere, but close to a pre-Beeching railway station
Into the old town, now all closed down, boarded up
Close to my abode
For cars didn't feature much then on the road
There was too much poverty and nobody owned much
Too much work, little play
But people seemed happier than they are today
Although it was winter and every day appeared to rain
There seemed to be an inner warmth that took away the pain
There was always a good fire burning
A newly slaughtered pig and roast potatoes for Sunday dinner
A walk down the country lane and everybody
Near and far seemed to know my name
Although I didn't know them
I went into a pub at Christmas and a lady at the bar said my name
And gave me the registration of my car with a twinkle in her eye
I was too astonished to reply
How did she know that? I thought
And then a Christmas drink at the bar I bought.

Philip Loudon

Memories

I sit alone and wonder
Why it should be so
That I hear so clearly voices
From past so long ago

Little ladies a-shouting
Who must be retiring men
Little lassies laughing
Who will never see sixty-one again.

I hear the songs of fishermen
Sailing out to sea
Melodies that dance bands play
When I was twenty-three.

Hymns the choir practised
In the centre village hall
Songs we sang when playing ball
Against the schoolhouse wall.

I hear the village old folk
Long sleeping in the grave
Talking of the good old days
Recall the good advice they gave.

Maybe it's my mind that's gone
Now I'm ninety-three
I'd better rise up and stir myself
And make a lovely cup of tea.

David Sheasby

My Mum's Day

Our mum is a real special person,
Of that I am more than positively certain,
She calls us in the morning, up with the lark,
Although we're sometimes still sleepy, we conjure a spark.

Breakfast on the table, kitchen nice and warm,
A welcome family gathering, to greet the dawn,
Our departure from home, and loveable Mum
We journey to school, teacher smiles a greeting,
I'm so glad you've come.

Through the course of the day, we think of our mum
Knowing she's at home, our friend, a real chum,
When it's time to leave school, Mum's at the school gate,
I can see her through the class window, I don't want to be late.

Mum often brings Toby, our loveable dog,
Toby's so pleased to see us, we make our way home with a happy jog
Once we are home we all have a wee snack,
Toby, as well, he just wags his tail, he knows it's time to relax.

What's new, we all sit and watch on TV,
I sit with my mum, so snug and warm, till it's time for our tea,
When tea is over, Mum gives me a warm bath,
Then I'm wrapped in a warm towel, then we giggle and laugh.

Mum then calls, 'Off we go then into your room.'
She turns back the covers, then we both notice the moon,
I leap into bed, with my teddy held oh so tight,
My lovely mum tucks me in, gives me a hug
Then kisses me goodnight.

I close my eyes tightly, with teddy by my side
And whisper a thank you to Heaven
For being my lovely mum's child.

Lorna Tippett

Digbeth Streets

Run! Run!
Down past the Old Wharf Tavern
Where Da and uncle are having a beer.
Past the railway arches
Eerily forbidding,
Like buttressed cathedrals of dark brick
The stench of the old knacker's yard
Pursuing us
Like death in stink manifested.

Drunken laughter.
Irish voices in song float by
Disembodied
Chasing us too as we skittered on
Through drizzle, thick and clinging
Fugitives from Auntie Peggy's watchful eye.

Into the night! Not allowed.
Not for children the slick cobbles
And the wash house door
Hanging open. A dark maw to swallow us,
We mere escaped morsels to be devoured.

Chickens clucked in the backyard
Evil demons from Hell to chase us home, we thought.
Creeping outside, excitement and terror mixed.
Backs to the wall.
She'll catch us. She will! There'll be trouble.

But easily faced compared to the outside.
The dark, the streets forbidden,
Where we, in our first new defiance
Had so hair-raisingly raced.

Miki Byrne

Simple Pleasures

When flicking through the photograph album,
Remembered marvellous places I'd seen.
The adventures I had there and then some,
Paddling in the sea, climbing hills - grass green.

Looking at days gone by, made me quite sad,
Then was not old, unsteady on my feet.
Long for the days, when I was young, bit mad,
Loved newspaper wrapped fish and chips - real treat.

Aware, nowadays, rarely leave my home,
I smile at a snap of me on donkey spot.
Spend days alone - offspring from here have flown,
Recall school hols with each day, sunny, hot.

S Mullinger

Yesteryear 1930s

My childhood was in yesteryear
I can recall it well
So carefree, happy, full of cheer
My thoughts quite often dwell.

The motorcars were very few
So we played on the street
We'd jump a rope, play hopscotch too
And race with nimble feet.

At certain times it was the trend
To play with bowlers, good
Some made of iron that did not bend
And others made of wood.

We'd race along and laugh and whoop
To school or any way
With stick or iron we'd drive our hoop
A lovely game to play.

Then time came round for spinning top
Fine specimens were had
We'd whip them with a leather crop
A bootlace, 'pinched' from Dad.

A paper chase or tallyho
Across ploughed field and grass
We'd race away, the hours would go
How quickly they did pass.

On summer days when school was through
Across the fields we'd roam
To 'clumps' or 'wheelpits', lodges too
Then, weary, turn for home.

Indoors we played with games and toys
Like tiddlywinks or cards
Lead soldiers in a fort for boys
Girls knitting yards and yards.

Paint pictures in a picture book
Play hoopla or 'I Spy'
Catch paper fish with magnet hook
Hunt thimble by and by.

There was a land of make-believe
Like castles made of chairs
Tall stories there we'd sit and weave
Till time to climb the stairs.

A fleeting glimpse of times so good
Which memory holds quite dear
A peep into my childhood
And happy yesteryear.

D J Wooding

Shirley

Mam first got ill when I was ten
My best friend at school was Shirley Raywood.
We were sworn blood sisters
Mingling our blood from cut knees in the playground.

I were in top juniors when a boy
Called John Warburton's mam died.
'Any of you could've been in the same boat'
Teacher said the morning it happened.

The morning mine went off in the ambulance
I thought it were my turn, but Shirley said,
'She can't die of a nervous breakdown, my mam says.'

After that it were all right
Every day we went to Shirley's house
In our lunch hour and ate her mam's fruit cake.

Rosemary Benzing

Down Memory Lane

How I love to often return
To those, what seem, unlike the present
Magical, happy days of yore
In reality, perhaps not always,
But in mind they always burn.

Sweet sixteen, first love, wonderment
War coming, fear, causing separation.
Food scarce, getting used to bombs
Rather blasé, you decide to enlist
Years later, peace returns, contentment.

Marriage, children, life ordinary again.
Family grow up, leave, you stay together.
Travel, marvel at sights, peaceful
Growing older, love just as pleasant.
You settle to routine, happily, memories remain.

Without warning, ageing, the dye is cast
Limbc get stiff, a cane is used
Still you enjoy living for
Always lurking, are your memories
To sustain your love of now and the past.

Marjorie Busby

Dad's Star

Billions of stars, shining so bright
In the dark, ink-coloured sky each night
Always present, though not always seen
Clouds covering the black, special dream.

One of those stars, a diamond, I know
Represents my dad - shining, aglow
He passed away, February 2001
That was when the star watching began.

The night of his death, planet Venus appeared
Bright, spectacular - and to it I neared
Drawn by its beauty, twinkling so clear
Significant, meaningful or a dad so dear.

Comfort was instant - just knowing he's there
Watching over us, showing his care
The star, it remained, for over a week
Giving peace, where needed, when time was bleak.

Blinking, colours, a spectrum of hue
In a vast expanse of night sky so blue
And Dad's star is more prominent of all
The blanket of the universe, how it does enthral.

I look to the heavens, every clear night
And the dot-to-dot wilderness is a beautiful sight
Even when clouds cover the picturesque view
I imagine Dad's star, because my mind sees it too.

Joanne Hale

Brief Encounter 1978

Brief Encounter 1978
My Welsh dream lost
Deirdre Mcguire
Met back in 1978
At Ty'r Felin reception centre
Bangor, Wales
I was there on a short holiday
There she was a Welsh dream
Beautiful brown hair and eyes
Beautiful sparkling smile for sure an angel
We looked at each other
Hit it off in an instant
For the period of time
I was at Ty'r Flein
We were always together
Deirdre Mcguire
For sure an angel
After leaving we kept in touch
But that's life, she left Ty're Felin
I believe moved to Hollyhead
But I left where I was
We lot contact
Just not found contact since
But I've never forgot her
My Welsh dream lost
Brief Encounter 1979
The beautiful angel girl
Deirdre Mcguire.

David J Hall

Oh, The Joy Of Being Young

Oh, what simple fun we had
In those ancient days, when just a lad
One thing that brought us to our knees
Was to see a dog scratching for fleas.

Oh, what simple fun we had
We were always happy, never ad
At noon we'd place snails in a line
The race would finish about half-past nine!

Oh, what simple fun we had
Always well-behaved, never bad
Cats arching their backs, we'd hear them hiss
A ringside seat, was hard to miss.

Oh, what simple fun we had
I'd say boisterous, never mad
Day after day, playing knock down ginger
Then hiding until hearing a moaning whinger.

Oh, what simple fun we had
In wintertime, when warmly clad
Throwing snowballs, endangering lives
Passing drivers would offer a bunch of fives!

Oh, what simple fun we had
When out of sigh of dear old dad
Throwing stinkbombs into an enclosed space
The windows would open at a furious pace!

Oh, what simple fun we had
To see the back of us, girls were glad
Showing them spiders in a matchbox
Or trying to pass on our chickenpox!

Oh, what simple fun we had
In ancient days when just a lad
Little things which would annoy
But it brought us so much joy.

B W Ballard

Anchor Books Information

We hope you have enjoyed reading this book - and that you will continue to enjoy it in the coming years.

If you like reading and writing poetry drop us a line, or give us a call, and we'll send you a free information pack.

Alternatively if you would like to order further copies of this book or any of our other titles, then please give us a call or log onto our website at www.forwardpress.co.uk

Anchor Books Information
Remus House
Coltsfoot Drive
Peterborough
PE2 9JX

(01733) 898102